What Every Believ
SPIRITUAL\WARFARE
second edition

What Every Believer Should Know About Spiritual Warfare
© Copyright Marcus Warner 2009 and 2020

All rights reserved. No portion of this book may be reproduced, stored in a retrieval system, or transmitted in any form or by any means—electronic, mechanical, photocopy, recording, scanning, or other—except for brief quotations in critical reviews or articles, without the prior written permission of the publisher.

Unless otherwise noted, Scriptures are taken from:

Holy Bible, New International Version®, NIV® Copyright ©1973, 1978, 1984, 2011 by Biblica, Inc.® Used by permission. All rights reserved worldwide.

The Holy Bible, English Standard Version. ESV® Text Edition: 2016. Copyright © 2001 by Crossway Bibles, a publishing ministry of Good News Publishers.

Published by Deeper Walk International.

Second Edition October, 2020

First printed in the United States of America

ISBN: 978-1-7327510-5-7

Deeper Walk International
13295 Illinois St. #223
Carmel, IN 46032

www.DeeperWalkInternational.org

Contents

Introduction	7
Chapter 1 – The Reality of Spiritual Warfare	9
Chapter 2 – Permission	17
Chapter 3 – Authority	31
Chapter 4 – The Process	45
Chapter 5 – Demons and Deception	59
Chapter 6 – The Occult	71
Appendix 1 – Freedom Prayers	89
Appendix 2 – Theological Note: The Role of Experience	93
Appendix 3 – Mark Bubeck's Round-up Prayer	101
About the Author & Deeper Walk	105
Go Deeper: Recommended Reading	107
Appreciations	109

Introduction

> Our first priority is to know God, but if we are really at war with a clever, experienced enemy, we need to know as much as we can about him.
> . . . Not to know how your enemy thinks and how he acts is to give your enemy a strategic advantage over you.
> Timothy M. Warner

I recently received a text from a good friend in which he shared the testimony of a young lady who had experienced dramatic freedom through deliverance. The young woman had been hospitalized more than once for suicidal thoughts and an eating disorder. She was a Christian and had been in therapy for quite some time. Along the way, she had learned lots of coping skills, but no one took seriously the idea that there could be demons involved with her struggles. When my friends met with her, they used tools they had learned from Deeper Walk to explore the possibility of demonic involvement. It didn't take long. She heard demonic voices in her head answer their questions. They were able to help this lady identify and evict a spirit of death and a spirit of anorexia that was causing her eating disorder. The next day, she sent them a text that said, "I feel like me again. No suicidal thoughts. No ED [Eating Disorder]. Just peace and joy. . . . Hallelujah! He reigns!"

A few months later, her freedom is still the new reality in which she lives. In a follow up text, my friend wrote, "We have to get [spiritual warfare ministry] accepted by the church somehow." It is sad that in spite of seeing thousands of people find freedom from strongholds through the years, too many churches either ignore the issue of Christians and demons or actively oppose it. Some churches that do practice spiritual warfare need greater balance and insight, but the biggest challenge seems to be to get Western Christians to take spiritual warfare seriously.

In this book you will be introduced to the basics you need to know in order to deal with most spiritual warfare situations that arise. There are more advanced topics that those who deal with warfare in more complex situations would need to know, but we will not be diving into the deep end in this book. The goal is to help you understand that the battle is real and learn the foundational perspectives, principles, and practices to help you begin winning life's battles.

Shallow end with this Book

One
The Reality of Spiritual Warfare

My experience with spiritual warfare began at the age of seven. I saw a demon in my dining room staring at me. It was a big, black thing with red eyes. As you can imagine, it freaked me out, and I started to scream. The others who were with me couldn't see it, but the thing was not just a vague image; it seemed to be physically present in the room. Since then I have met other children who have had night-time visitors and lived with paranormal activity in their homes. It should be noted that just because I saw the demon in this form, doesn't mean that demons always have this form. There is every reason to believe that they can assume forms for the purposes needed.

A friend once called me because his son was afraid to sleep in his room. It seemed he was seeing an old woman in a rocking chair show up from time to time. He wanted to know if I thought it was just the boy's imagination or if it could be a demonic manifestation. I told him that it could definitely be demonic and counseled him to cleanse the boy's room by renouncing any claim the enemy had to the house, commanding that any spirits assigned to the place or to his son leave, and inviting Jesus to fill the house and especially that room with His presence. Many years have since passed, and they have never had another issue with strange visitors in their house.

I spoke with a lady who is now in full-time Christian ministry who grew up in a haunted house where everyone in the family knew the ghost by name and treated him like part of the family. It was only years later that she came to learn about the reality of spiritual warfare and was able to make it leave.

A five year old boy was in bed one night, when an angel appeared and startled him. The young boy told it to leave. The angel asked him why, and the child answered, "Because in the Bible real angels always told people not to be afraid. Well, I'm scared to death, and you never said not to be afraid." Smart boy! (If only a few cult leaders had done the same thing!) At that, the angel turned into a hideous looking creature and said, "Would you rather I came looking like this?" and left.

I could tell you lots of stories like these. My question is, "Why do some kids get attacked and others don't?" How does this work? In my case, my parents had just been involved in their first deliverance session. A woman had sought help from a local Christian counselor because of compulsive behaviors that were negatively impacting her life. The counselor sensed there was something more going on than a battle with the flesh and referred her to my mom and dad.

As they talked with this woman, they discovered that she had received the gift of tongues several years before. It was a precious gift to her, but her compulsions began about the time someone had laid hands on her. My parents tested her "gift" by asking the spirit if Jesus Christ was the Lord of all who had come in the flesh. When they did this, a deep voice spoke through the lady that said, "I'm strong. You can't get me." It didn't take much discernment to realize this wasn't the Holy Spirit! It did, however, take a manifestation that dramatic to convince this woman her tongue could possibly be false.

The problem was that she struggled with inferiority and felt insecure in her relationship with Christ. Her "gift" was her anchor that let her know she was accepted and important to God. But the gift of tongues was never meant to be the proof that we were accepted by God. Our complete and unconditional acceptance was purchased for us by the blood of Christ. Our confidence is to be in the person of Christ and His finished work on our behalf. Gaining freedom from the demonic spirit and learning about her true identity in Christ helped this woman gain victory over the problems that had taken her to a counselor in the first place. The adversary, however, was not very happy.

The demon that I saw in my house showed up the week after my parents' encounter with this wicked spirit. It was an act of intimidation. My dad put it this way. Satan was offering him a deal: "You leave me alone and I'll leave you alone. And you better leave me alone because if you don't, look what I can do to your kids!" The devil was trying to get at my parents through me. Thankfully, my parents were wise and courageous enough to realize that you do not make deals with the devil. You resist him. My parents began to teach me how to fight by using Scripture and praying in the name of Jesus. The demon came back one night, but I was prepared, and it was quickly evicted. Who knew that resisting the devil would work better than screaming and hiding?

Pastors and Spiritual Warfare

Sadly, too few Christians are trained for war. It is even difficult to find pastors who know what to do with the enemy. Our seminaries and Bible colleges rarely deal with this subject in a practical way, and many actually teach dangerously untrue paradigms about spiritual warfare that warn people away from involvement with the subject.

A young, bi-vocational pastor was called to the home of a woman in crisis. He went with his mentor, a pastor with over thirty years of ministry experience. When they arrived, they found the woman curled up on the floor in a catatonic state. The veteran pastor sized up the situation, excused himself, and took the young pastor into the next room.

"Do you know what that was?" the veteran asked.

"No," replied the young pastor.

"You were looking into the eyes of a demon."

"Well, what do we do?"

"We leave. They will call an ambulance, get her checked into a psych ward, and in a few days she'll be okay."

Can you believe it? The only solution this veteran pastor had to offer was to get her checked into a psych ward and just walk away. He had no idea how to help because he had been taught Christians couldn't have experiences like this, and so no one had trained him how to help.

On one occasion, I received a phone call from another young pastor who was facing a crisis. It turned out there was a person in his office rolling around on the floor with demonic noises emanating through her (I could hear the sounds in the background as we talked). This pastor had been trained at a nationally recognized seminary, but nothing in his training had prepared him for this. I asked what steps he had already taken, and he said, "I commanded the demon to leave in the name of Jesus, but with no effect." He had also tried reading Scripture out loud, but it had only made the situation worse. I felt sorry for him because he really had no idea what to do.

"It looks like you need a crash course on spiritual warfare," I said. "Authority alone won't work. Simply commanding the demon to leave without removing its right to be there will just leave you worn out and discouraged. Instead, use your authority to bind the demons in the name of Jesus. Command them to be silent and inactive and to allow you to speak to the woman who came to you for help."

I listened as the pastor did this, and I could hear the room get quiet. She had stopped acting out. He was soon able to speak with the woman directly. When a demon interrupted him, he bound it again and continued. He learned quickly.

I then told him that this kind of demonic episode usually only happens if there has been significant occult involvement by the person themselves or their family. I encouraged him to ask if this woman had ever dabbled in the occult. It turned out that he knew this woman well. She was actually a relative of his wife. He knew she had been raised in a family where the occult was commonly practiced and that she had often participated in tarot card readings, Ouija boards, and other forms of witchcraft.

I explained that all of these occult sins needed to be renounced and the demons commanded to leave. They had permission to be there because of these sins, so the sins needed to be confessed and rejected in order to get rid of that permission.

To his credit, the pastor handled the situation beautifully. Once he got the basic concepts in mind of using authority to bind, renouncing the sins that had opened the door to the demons, and assisting the woman to use her own authority in Christ to evict them, they started making headway. After walking through the process with me a few times, he said, "I think I see how this works. I'll call you back if I need any more help."

He called me back a few days later and said that over the course of two sessions they had covered a lot of ground, and he believed the woman was completely free of the demons. He was now discipling her in order to build her up in the faith. However, he had two very good questions, "Why was I taught that stuff like this can't happen to Christians?" And, "Where do I go to learn how to help people in this condition?"

I was able to direct him to Mark Bubeck's book *The Adversary* and to one co-authored by my father and Neil Anderson, now titled *The Essential Guide to Spiritual Warfare*. A few months later he and his wife came to one of our training courses and told me about the many victories they were beginning to see and how much he was growing as he continued on this journey.

Born into War

Spiritual warfare is not an optional activity for believers. You have not been granted immunity or vaccinated against the effects of the devil by an injection of the Holy Spirit. Although you may never be confronted with a demon in your house or in someone you are discipling, wouldn't it be a good idea to know what to do if you are?

Even if spiritual warfare never visits you in such dramatic ways as some of the stories I have shared, you live with it every day in the battles you do experience, like the battle for your mind, the battle for your church, the battle for your home, and the battle for your community. It is time for the church to wake up to the reality of the war and to prepare its people and its leaders for battle.

We were born into the middle of a great, cosmic conflict that affects every area of life. As Christians, we really have only two options. We can live in fear and ignorance or we can learn to fight. So, where in the Bible does it say, "Ignore the devil, and he will leave you alone"? Nowhere! It warns us repeatedly, "Be alert! Be prepared! Put on your armor! Resist!" These are not passive words. We are called to be intentional and diligent in preparing ourselves for battle. This book is meant to get you started on that journey.

Discussion Questions

1. What dangers do you see in studying spiritual warfare?

2. What dangers do you see in <u>not</u> studying spiritual warfare? *you will not recognize Satan. the Demon.*

3. What questions did this chapter raise for you? (Write them down and see how many get answered as you read the rest of the book). *What forms could they be In.*

4. Have you had any experiences that led you to believe in the reality of spiritual warfare? Did you get any resolution to those experiences?

5. What issues do you hope this book will address? *Identifying & Dealing with Demons.*

Personal Exercise

Here are two sample prayers that you can start using, possibly on a daily basis. One is an evening prayer, and one is a morning prayer.

Evening Prayer

Father in heaven,

Thank You for Your provision for every need I have faced and will face. Thank You for Your promises to work all things together for good in my life and that goodness and love will follow me all the days of my life.

As we quiet our hearts and minds for the night to sleep, I ask for Your peace to be on our home and all who are in it. I ask You to surround us with Your holy angels and hedge of protection. I ask You to sweep the house clean of any spiritual presence that should not be here and replace it with Your own comforting presence.

In the name of Jesus, Amen.

Morning Prayer

You are El Elyon (the Most High God), I will worship no other god but You. You are Yahweh Sabaoth (the commander of the hosts of heaven), be my protector from every device of the evil one. You are Jehovah Jireh (Yawheh Yireh—my provider) provide for my needs today. You are the Good Shepherd, guide me and give me ears to recognize Your voice today.

The idea is not to make these the only prayers you say, but to add them to whatever else you pray. Do this for a week and notice if you see anything change.

Two
Permission

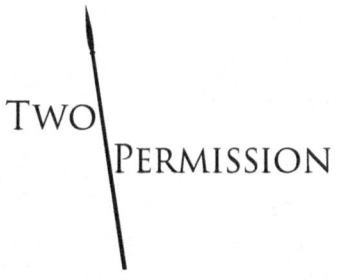

A few years ago, I was hiking on a trail in the Cascade Mountains with my son. I saw a log that had fallen across the path and remembered something I had heard in a sermon years before. The pastor had grown up in Alabama where they have a lot of snakes. He had said he was taught at an early age, "Never step over a log when you are out hiking. Always step on it, then jump across because snakes like to sleep in the shade."

With this in mind, I told my son to step on top of the log and jump. When I got to the log, I did the same thing. When I looked back, I was thankful for the Holy Spirit's prompting because, sure enough, there was a long, bluish-grey snake stretched out alongside the log.

Now, my son and I did not go on a walk that day to hunt for snakes. I wasn't even thinking about them. But common sense dictates that if you are going into an area where snakes often live, you might want to learn something about them so that you can avoid them if possible and know what to do if you run into one.

It is the same with demons. I don't live my life fixated on them, but I know they are out there. I also know where I am most apt to run into them and what to do if it happens. They are most often found in moments of temptation, in occult activity, in unresolved sin, in bitterness, in church factions, and in the glittering appeal of both worldly and Christian counterfeits of true spirituality.

The Throne Room

Several times in Scripture we get glimpses into the throne room of heaven where God is surrounded by heavenly beings. In this throne room, God issues decrees and initiates activity on the earth. As the king above all kings, God is sovereign. This means everyone in heaven and on earth and under the earth answers to Him. It also means He is free to do whatever He wants. Fortunately for us, what God wants is good, righteous, and just. He hates evil and holds those who do evil to account.

The reality of the throne room helps us understand the foundations of spiritual warfare.

- Warfare is limited to this present evil age. It began with a revolt in heaven. It will end when Jesus returns and brings this present age to an end. Thus, the book of Revelation records a scene in the throne room in which Jesus—the Lamb—opens the seals of the scroll that contains the decree for bringing this age to an end.
- This war is about the throne. Satan wants to replace the Most High as the functional king of the universe. We see this in the temptation of Jesus in which the devil wanted Jesus to bow down to him. He was essentially offering Jesus the number two position. This is also alluded to in Isaiah's taunt against the king of Babylon.

  > You said in your heart, "I will ascend to the heavens; I will raise my throne above the stars of God; I will sit enthroned on the mount of assembly . . . (14:13-14 NIV)"

  Two observations related to this text need highlighted. One, the king of Babylon addressed here may not be merely human. The Babylonian kings were worshiped and were said to have descended from the gods. It is possible that this is not simply a taunt of the current king in Isaiah's day, but of the ultimate king of Babylon—the original fallen angel who made that city his home. Two, it is worth noting that the idea of a son of the high God taking the throne from his father is a common theme in nearly all pagan mythology. It seems to reflect Satan's own agenda. He knows he is not the creator, but he believes he has a plan to take the throne.

- While Satan wants the throne, he does not have it. Yahweh sits on the throne. Jesus sits at His right hand waiting for the day when this age ends, and He unites heaven and earth together in one family under one king.

- From His throne, God has laid down rules for this contest over who will rule humanity. He has granted Satan and his kingdom tremendous freedom. He has also granted humans tremendous freedom. But neither group has unlimited freedom. There are clear boundaries for this conflict established in heaven.

- Jesus is God's champion in this war. Every test failed by man and angels, Jesus faced and overcame. He is the victor and has been given all authority in heaven and on earth. Now He waits for God to make His enemies a footstool for His feet. The throne will be given to Jesus forever and ever.

- Satan knows the throne belongs to Jesus, but he is working feverishly to turn the nations against Jesus. He wants to rule the world that God created. Just as the devil tried to prevent God from sending the promised "seed of woman" who would crush his head, and just as he fortified Canaan to prevent God from fulfilling His promise to give the land to Israel—through whom the promised seed would come, so now he is working hard to bring all nations under his control to try to prevent the rule of Christ on earth. Victory for the enemy would be a scenario in which all of the people of earth choose him as their king and reject God's Messiah. In Psalm 2, God mocks all of these plans. He has decreed that they will fail, just as the devil failed to stop the coming of the Messiah, he will fail to prevent His rule on earth.

> Why do the nations conspire, and the peoples plot in vain? The kings of the earth rise up and the people band together against Yahweh and against His Messiah saying, "Let us break their chains and throw off their shackles." The one enthroned in heaven laughs; the Lord scoffs at them. He rebukes them in His anger and terrifies them in His wrath.[1]

At this point in the Psalm, God throws down the gauntlet. He tells all who are in rebellion against Him His plan and dares them to stop it. His plan is to install the Messiah as king over all nations. This will happen, He says. He then advises them to "Kiss the Son"–Jesus—lest He be angry with them. This theme of God's judgment on the angels who have rebelled against Him and attempted to establish themselves as gods who rule without regard to Him is an important thread that runs throughout Scripture.

At the individual level, when it comes to our personal battles for freedom from the devil's snares and deceptions, the throne room helps us understand two core principles on which spiritual warfare ministry is based: permission and authority.

---

1 | Author's translation.

Permission

The idea of permission flows from the reality of God's sovereignty. From the perspective of the courtroom of heaven, demons need permission to do whatever they do. At the beginning of this age, God decreed that Satan and his demons were free to roam the earth. However, they are not free to do whatever they want to do, or we would all be dead—or at least enslaved. Satan had to get permission to attack Job (Job 1-2). He had to ask to "sift" Peter (Luke 22:31).

You might wonder why God would ever give demons permission to do anything. But the Fall of Man had real consequences, as did the rebellion of the angels. The day will come when God will bring this age to an end and the kingdom of darkness will be destroyed. This is why we pray, "Come quickly, Lord Jesus."

Demons gain the right to greater influence and control when they are given permission by people. This is one of the reasons idolatry is such a serious crime. It extends the right of the demons represented by the idols to greater influence not only in the life of the individual worshiper, but in the cultures that embrace these idols and the gods they represent.

In the battle for personal freedom, there are several common ways demons gain permission to a place in our lives. They can be remembered with the word SOUL-L (as in, there is a battle for your soul).

- **S**in. When we justify our sin and do not confess it, the devil gets a foothold—which is a beachhead for greater access into our lives (Ephesians 4:26-27). As both Jesus and Paul taught, whoever sins is a slave of sin.
- **O**ccult. Spiritual power that does not come from God is occult. When we participate in activity in which we seek the secret knowledge and power of

occult practices, we establish fellowship with demons (1 Corinthians 10:22—see also the list of forbidden occult activity in Deuteronomy 18:9-13).

- **Unforgiveness.** Bitterness creates bondage that can end in torment (Matthew 18:21-35).

- **Lies.** Lies we believe leave us in the control of the deceiver. As the father of lies (John 8:44) the devil uses deception to drive emotions that lead to foolish behavior. One of the most common problems caused by Satan's lies is anxiety.

- **Lineage.** When members of our family tree do things that give demons permission to a place in our family line, those demons work to keep their right to that family from one generation to the next. The Bible is filled with examples of how sin can have generational consequences. One of those consequences is that many of us are born into a battlefield because of the family we are in, which means the demons have greater permission to be active in our lives.

Later in this book, we will talk about how to remove the permission opened by these doorways and evict the unwanted spirits. For now, I just want to emphasize the importance of permission and authority.

Territorial Spirits. The principle of permission also applies to cultures and territories. Whole populations who live in a particular region (such as a country, province, or district) can give permission for greater activity to demons when their leaders enter into covenants with false gods or when the authority structure in that culture agrees with the devil's will rather than God's. When Moab chose to make Chemosh its god (Numbers 21:29), it gave the demons associated with that powerful spirit permission to a far greater degree of activity in their country than they would have had without the idolatry of the people. In the same way, individuals—even

Christians—can make choices that give demons a legal right to be active in their lives.

If a demon has a legal right to be somewhere, you can't just come along and say, "In the name of Jesus, you have to leave." It would be like trying to evict someone from a house who has a contract giving them a legal right to be there. If you want to get rid of them, you have to remove the legal ground they claim.

People who find themselves in long shouting matches with demons that drag on for hours have trouble because they are trying to evict a demon that has a legal right to be where it is. No amount of shouting "In the name of Jesus, I command you to leave" is going to make it leave.

Most of what happens in a biblically-balanced, practical approach to deliverance takes place at the level of removing legal ground. Once that is done, the evicting is generally much easier. Removing legal ground is essentially a matter of confessing sins, forgiving debts, or renouncing lies, and then canceling the permission given these have given to the enemy.

Authority

Authority is the right to represent power. As Christians, we have the right to represent the kingdom of God in this world. It is the power of the kingdom that makes spiritual warfare winnable, not our own personal strength or godliness.

In order to understand spiritual warfare, it can help to think in legal terms. When it comes to permission, we need to do the work of a lawyer. Lawyers deal with contracts and agreements. One of the tasks we do in warfare ministry is to help people cancel the agreements they have made with the devil that have given him permission to a place in their lives. They need legal advice and help to get free from the spiritual contracts that have ensnared them.

In regard to authority, we need to do the work of a police officer. Our job is to enforce the laws of the kingdom of heaven. Police officers have the authority to represent the power of the government. Their authority is not absolute or unlimited, but, within the limits established by law, it is real. When you see an officer, it doesn't really matter if that person is male or female, black or white, crude or kind; if you break the law, they have the authority to give you a ticket or arrest you. If I see the flashing lights of a police car behind me when I'm driving, I don't wait to see if I know the officer or respect the person's character before I pull over. I respect the uniform and the authority it represents. I know that the officer represents the power of the government and this is not a question of who the better or stronger person is; it is a question of authority.

Demons understand authority. They know that, as a Christian, I represent the power of the kingdom of God and that, when they cross me, it is not really a question of whether I am stronger, or they are stronger. I know that in most cases they are stronger. You never want to make a confrontation with a demon about how righteous, smart, or spiritual you are. It is not about your strength. It is about the power of the kingdom you represent and the power of Christ Himself. Demons know they are risking the wrath of the kingdom when they mess with a Christian. However, they are counting on the fact that most Christians have no idea how to exercise their authority in Christ. They also know if a Christian has surrendered legal ground and what that gives them permission to do.

Christians and Demons

The question is often asked, "How can a Christian have a demon?" It is really not that difficult of a question to answer, if you get the right paradigm in place.

Part of the problem is the language we use to discuss the issue. Most theology books talk about demonic activity as possession, oppression, or temptation. However, the word *possession* never occurs in the original languages. One of the reasons it came into common use is that the translators of the King James Version used "possession" to interpret the Greek word *daimonizomai*. This word is the verbal form of the noun *daimon*—which means "demon." There is nothing in the Greek word that implies possession. Possession refers to ownership, and Christians are "owned" by the Lord Jesus Christ who bought us with His blood. Christians cannot be "possessed" in this sense of the word.

To overcome this translation challenge, many have suggested translating this verb as "demonize." The advantage of this term is that it does not imply ownership and can be thought of as a scale of influence. In this sense, Christians can be demonized because they can give the devil permission to a place of influence in their lives. Let me share three word pictures of how this works.

1. **The Temple.** Just as humans have a body, mind, and heart (or spirit) so the temple has an outer court, an inner court, and an inner sanctum—the Holy of Holies. In Ezekiel 8-10 we see how it is possible for demons to be admitted into the outer courts of the temple at the same time that God is dwelling in the innermost room. This picture helps us understand that Christ can dwell in our hearts (our Holy of Holies) while our flesh and our mind permit demonic activity.

    Ezekiel's vision began at the north gate of the temple, where an idol (most likely an Asherah pole) greeted the worshipers as they entered. In the outer court, he saw the seventy elders of Israel offering incense to pagan gods (8:10-12). He also saw the women of Israel performing the ritual mourning for Tammuz (a Babylonian god whose mythological story has him dying in battle only to be raised to life by his consort Ishtar; similar to the mythological stories of Baal and Anat in Canaan and of Osiris and Isis in Egypt). It was believed that performing the mourning rituals would bring blessing and fertility to the land and families of the worshipers (8:13-14).

Next, Ezekiel was shown the Holy Place, where only priests were allowed to enter. The prophet saw twenty-five men bowing down to the sun in worship (8:15-16). Outside the temple, the city itself was filled with violence and perversion (8:17-18).

While all of this was going on, the Shekinah glory (Gods' presence) was still in the Holy of Holies. In chapter 10 we read that the Glory of the Lord left the temple, but only after it had been filled with demonic abominations (10:18-19). This means that God was present in the temple at the same time that demons were being summoned into the outer courts. Can you see how God's presence and the unholy presence of demonic entities could be in the same temple at the same time? God was present in the innermost court, while, in the outer courts, demons were being summoned by the rituals being performed.

It is the same with Christians. God's Spirit may live in our hearts, but that does not mean we cannot give a place for demons to reside in our flesh or build strongholds in our minds.

2. **Rental Property.** Dr. Karl Payne has written an excellent book called *Spiritual Warfare: Christians, Demonization, and Deliverance*. He has written several books on discipleship and apologetics, served as the

chaplain of the Seattle Seahawks for nearly two decades, and has over thirty years of experience in deliverance ministry. We have often taught together on the subject of spiritual warfare and have become friends. In his book, Karl uses the imagery of rental property to explain how a Christian can give space to a demon in their lives. In this picture, Jesus owns the house (our lives), but we serve as the landlord. We are stewards of the house. If we refuse to allow Jesus to be lord in an area of our lives, we open a door for demons to move in. He writes,

> We essentially place a vacancy sign outside that says, "Rooms for Rent." Demonic spirits are more than willing to answer the ad. And once they have permission to rent one room, they will aggressively and simultaneously attempt to take control of other rooms, while inviting relatives to move in with them (174-175).

The idea that the Holy Spirit and wicked spirits cannot occupy the same space does not mean that Christians cannot have demons. Christians cannot be owned by demons as their possession, but they can open doors that give them a place to live.

3. **A Field.** My friend and colleague Daryl Anderson has often used a word picture to explain how we surrender legal ground to the devil. He learned the concept from a preacher years ago. According to this imagery, Jesus owns a plot of land (your life) and you as a Christian are the steward of the property. One day the devil comes along and offers to buy some "junk ground" that is being unproductive. He points out that it is worthless as it is and promises that if you give it to him, he can add a lot of fun to your life.

In a moment of weakness, you foolishly sign a contract to give him the right to live on a small bit of property. At first, nothing really bad happens. Your life doesn't fall apart, and it seems like maybe this will work out. You will have enough of Christ to go to heaven and enough of sin to have fun. But, after a couple of weeks, the devil comes back and complains that he has to trespass on your property in order to get to his. He proposes that you give him a small walking path. You are suspicious but grant him his request. Soon, he is back demanding that the path be widened. "You really don't expect me to dig a basement with a shovel, do you?" He has a point, and you relent to his demands. This seems to happen more and more frequently. He shames you into giving up more property and cons you into participating in darker activities than you anticipated.

This was not supposed to happen. You just wanted to have a little fun, and now it seems like someone else is running your life. You wake up and look around to realize your life is out of control and you wonder how you will ever get out of the mess you have made. (From *Heart to Heart Connections*, 19-21).

Conclusion

In the next few chapters we will talk about how to get out of such a mess. For now, my hope is that these analogies have helped you see how Christians can surrender "ground" in a way that gives the devil a legal right to a place in their lives even though the Holy Spirit lives within them. In his book *Waking the Dead*, John Eldredge writes that Satan wants us to enter into agreements with him that give him rights to be active in our lives.

The whole plan is based on agreements. When we make those agreements with the demonic forces suggesting things to us, we come under their influence. It becomes a kind of permission we give the enemy, sort of like a contract. The bronze gates start clanging shut around us. I'm serious—maybe half the stuff people are trying to 'work through' in counseling offices, or pray about in their quiet times, is simply agreements they've made with the Enemy (*Waking the Dead*, 154-155).

Can you see how a basic understanding of the devil's schemes in this area can help us recognize what is going on in our lives so that we can begin to fight it with the proper weapons and strategies?

Discussion Questions

1. This chapter covered a lot of ground—the throne room, permission, authority, and whether Christians can give a place to demons in their lives.

   - What insights stood out to you about the throne room?

   - How is the concept of permission foundational to spiritual warfare?

   - What did you learn about the believer's authority in this chapter?

   - Did the illustrations about Christians and demons make sense? Did it leave you with more questions, or leave you feeling satisfied?

2. What other takeaways did you get from this chapter?

Personal Exercise

This exercise is meant to start the process of living with more freedom by taking back legal ground from the enemy.

Father,

Will You show me one agreement I have made with the enemy that has surrendered legal ground and needs to be reclaimed? (*Write out the first agreement that comes to your mind. Ask the Lord to help you word it accurately.*)

In the name of Jesus, I ask You, Father, to forgive me for making this agreement. I hereby cancel it and ask You to strip it of any legal authority in the courtroom of heaven.

In the name of Jesus, I command any spirits who have had permission to a place in my life because of this agreement to leave now and take all of your works and effects with you.

I commit this area of my life to the lordship of Christ and ask You, Father, to cleanse and fill it with Your Spirit.

Amen.

Three
Authority

When I was a child my parents taught me to stand against harassment from wicked spirits by saying, "In the name of Jesus, I command you to leave." At the time, I felt like a sheriff out in the Wild West telling the bad guys, "Stop, in the name of the Law."

My parents explained to me that I was not standing against the demons in my own name or in my own power. I was standing against them in the name and power of Jesus in the same way that David stood against Goliath in the name and power of the Lord. If it was David against Goliath, Goliath would win every time. But it was Goliath against the Most High God. David was simply God's representative.

To act in the name of Jesus is to act within the boundaries of the authority He has delegated to us. To do something "in His name" is to do it as His representative in the same way that a sheriff represents the local government. As a child, it was obvious to me that the demons had more power than I did. If the contest was between my power and their power, they would win every time.

But when I came against the enemy in the name of Jesus, they had to listen because, if they chose to mess with me, they knew they were picking a fight with Jesus. It would be like me being pulled over by a police officer and saying, "Oh, it's just Joe. He's not a very good police officer and he's an even worse father and husband. I don't have to listen to him." His authority in that setting has nothing to do with his competence or his character. It has to do with the government he represents. If he is within the bounds of the law in his dealings with me, he has authority over me. In the same way, Christians are like police officers. Whether we are one day out of the academy or a thirty-year veteran, we all have the same authority. Some are just more experienced at using it.

The Christian's authority over demons is not a spiritual gift. Don't fall into the trap of thinking that some Christians have this authority, and some do not. The authority of the believer is rooted in the fact that we are in Christ, and in Christ we are seated with Him in the heavenly realms far above the angels, whether evil or elect. When Jesus defeated Satan at the cross and rose again, He was given a name above every name (Philippians 2:7-11). This is why Jesus told His disciples, "All authority in heaven and on earth has been given unto me" (Matthew 28:18-20). Our Lord has been given the highest position of authority in the universe. In Christ, a measure of that authority has been delegated to us to wield in harmony with His will and purposes.

Victor vs. Victim

The diagram in this section illustrates our position of authority. Humans were made "a little lower than the angels" (Psalm 8:5), so we have them on the bottom row with stars (representing the angels) on the second tier. One of the stars is upside down and dark to represents Satan and his demons since Revelation 12:4 references a third of the stars being swept from the sky by the dragon.

If I were to take on the Adversary in my own strength, he would be in a position of dominance over me. Unfortunately, many Christians live this way. It keeps us in the position of "victim." If we believe this to be true, it will rob us of one of our greatest resources and leave us defeated and discouraged. However, Jesus made Himself a little lower than the angels and became a human. Not only that, He made Himself our servant. What is more, He laid down His life for us and died for the sins of the whole world. In this way He disarmed the angelic hosts that were at war against Him. He defeated Satan and robbed him of the keys to death and Hades. He then rose to life and ascended to heaven where God seated Him far above all principalities and powers.[1] In Ephesians 2:6 we read that God raised us up together with Christ and seated us together with Him in heavenly places. From this position at the right hand of the Father we have intimacy with God and authority over the enemy. We no longer struggle as victims, but we wage war as victors.

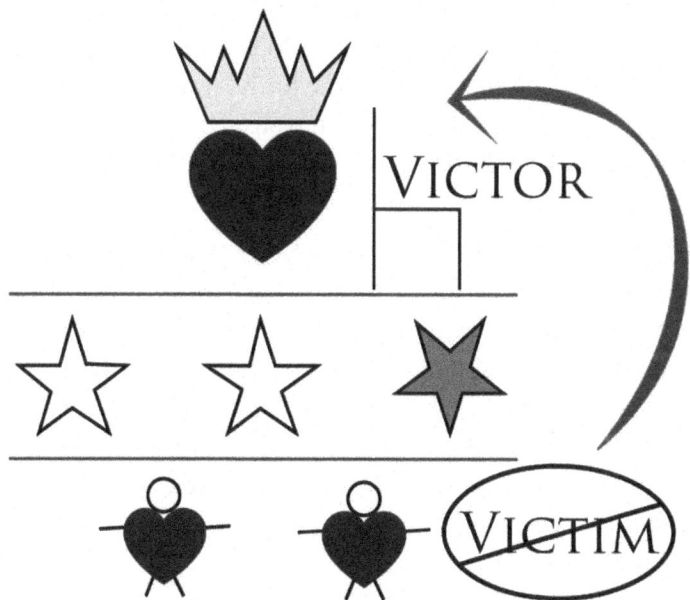

Common Errors About Authority

There are two errors into which Christians sometimes fall with regard to authority. First, there are those who believe that Christians have **NO** authority. These people often point

---

[1] | *Principalities* likely refers to the spirits who rule territories, such as the Prince of Persia (Daniel 10). *Powers* likely refers to spirits with power over various elements of nature, like wind, storms, sky, earth, etc.

to a text like Jude in which Michael did not rebuke Lucifer, but said, "The Lord rebuke you." They argue that if Michael, who is greater than we are, did not have authority over Lucifer, how could we? Now that you have seen the authority diagram of our position in Christ, how would you answer that question? Hopefully, you would recognize that Michael and Lucifer are equals in authority. The angels, even archangels, are not seated with Christ at the right hand of God the Father Almighty. It should also be pointed out that the humans discussed in Jude's letter are false teachers, who are not Christians at all, and therefore have no claim to authority. This passage should be understood in the context of an apostle who is "contending for the faith" against mockers who have infiltrated the flock like wolves in sheep's clothing. Jude's primary purpose is not to address the issue of authority but to point out the arrogance of these false teachers.

Second, there are those who believe that Christians have **ALL** authority. Our authority as Christians is limited by law. We do not have unlimited authority. If we did, we could just go into any hospital and say, "In the name of Jesus, everybody is healed." Or we could go to a Hindu temple and cast out all of the demonic spirits. If we spoke, it would be as if Jesus were speaking. But we can only use our authority to the limit that the decrees and laws of the courtroom of heaven allow us to use it.

For example, if a police officer pulls you over and says, "I'm sorry. You were going fifteen miles an hour over the speed limit, I have to give you a ticket," she has every right to that. But if the same officer pulls you over and says, "I'm sorry, but your breath stinks, I am giving you a ticket," well, she doesn't have the authority to do that. Her authority is limited by the law. If the law says there is a speed limit and you violate the limit, a police officer can give you a ticket; and if you resist her authority, you will find yourself fighting not just the officer but all the power of the government represented by the officer.

In the same way, I can use my authority over a demon if that demon is doing something it has no right to do. But if the demon has legal ground, I can't evict it simply because I feel like it. Before I can tell it to leave, I have to reclaim the surrendered ground. The next chapter will explain the process of how you do that.

Uses of Authority

When it comes to spiritual warfare, there are three primary uses of authority, (1) binding, (2) loosing, and (3) evicting. We bind the enemy, loose ourselves and others from the enemy, and evict the enemy. There is a time and place for each of these activities.

Binding. The Greek word "binding" is *deo* and "loosing" is *luo*. *Deo* is normally used for securing prisoners by tying them with ropes or putting them in irons. It was also used of binding together sheaves of grain. Jesus said that we sometimes must bind the strongman in order to rob his house (Matthew 12:29). In spiritual warfare, we do this by using our authority to bind the enemy so that the person we are trying to help can function enough to express their will. Many times, I have seen people who were unable to complete their prayers or verbalize their renunciations of the legal ground being claimed by the enemy until that enemy was bound in the name of Jesus.

A young man once came see me who was struggling in his attempts to disciple a friend. Even though he had years of experience in discipling others through the campus ministry he helped to lead, he wasn't having any success with his friend.

"I don't get it," he said. "This man is a veterinarian. He's smart, he's successful, but whenever we talk about the Bible, he can't seem to follow the simplest line of thought. I've tried everything." Then he looked at me with a look of understanding and added, "Except spiritual warfare." He asked me what to do.

I told him, "The next time you meet with this man, during your opening prayer, bind any demons from interfering with his ability to process what he is learning or any work that God wants to do." He wasn't sure how to do that; so I let him know that it was as simple as saying the words, "In the name of Jesus, I bind any demons from interfering." He said he would give it a try.

The next Sunday at church, he came up to me with a look of amazement on his face. "You won't believe it," he said. "Not only did my friend interact intelligently with the study this time, we found out that his family has been practicing the occult for generations and that he has secretly practiced homosexuality for over seven years." That made sense. Both of those things would give legal ground to the enemy to harass this man. "So, what do I do now?" my friend asked. I pointed him to Neil Anderson's book *The Bondage Breaker* and told him to take his friend through *The Steps to Freedom in Christ*.

That day, this young man who was an expert in discipling others according to the traditional discipling models started a journey of his own that opened up areas in his own life in which he was living in bondage and needing to be free. I was able to take him through the *Steps to Freedom* as well and help him get grounded in the basics of heart-focused discipleship.

There are many times when I am helping someone work through their baggage that we get interference from the enemy. I routinely stop and bind demons from interfering before we move on. It is amazing how dramatic the change can be.

Once, a lady was in the midst of forgiving someone for sexually abusing her when a black box appeared and blocked her memory of the event. We both thought that was odd, so I led her to pray, "In the name of Jesus, if this black box is from the enemy to interfere with what we are doing, I command them to remove it now and to stop interfering." Immediately, the black box disappeared, and she completed a time with the Lord that led to great healing in her heart.

Another time, a person was having trouble getting the words out when he was renouncing his involvement with the occult. He would start to say, "I renounce S——," but he couldn't get the rest of it out. (I have actually seen this dozens of times.) We simply paused and bound the demons that were interfering, and he was able to finish his prayer.

Once you deal with this often enough, you learn to simply open your sessions with prayer binding the enemy to inactivity and to obedience to the commands of Christ. A good and very thorough model for such a prayer can be found in Karl Payne's book *Spiritual Warfare*.

Loosing. Christians use binding to restrict demons. We use loosing to cancel agreements and assignments. To loosen is to undo a bond. It is removing the cords that demons have used to keep people in bondage. A common example of this is forgiveness. Forgiving removes the bonds of bitterness that keep us spiritually connected to someone who has wronged us. We can also practice loosing by canceling "soul ties." A soul tie is a demonic bond that connects two people together. It is usually formed by the shared experience of sin. It may be that the people sinned together, perhaps by engaging in sex outside of marriage or by committing a crime together. But it may also be that one person sinned against another through abuse or some other unwanted behavior.

A friend of mine—let's call him John—was explaining soul ties to a buddy of his who had engaged in sexual relations with several women during his lifetime. Now that he was married, he was having trouble not thinking about other women when he was with his wife, and he was struggling with lust in general. John told him to make a list of all the women with whom he had been sexually inappropriate and renounce any soul ties that had been formed with them. Once he was done, he advised him to command any demons to leave that were keeping him bound to them.

The next time John met with his friend, the man said that he had significantly more freedom from breaking those soul ties. However, he confided there was one woman with whom it didn't seem to work. As John listened to his friend, the word "idol" kept coming to mind. He asked, "If I were to use the word 'idol' about this woman, would that make sense to you?" The friend immediately said yes. He realized that as a young man, he had worshiped her as if she were a goddess. She was his dream girl. He not only had to renounce his sexual activity with her, he had to renounce the idolatry that had created a second soul tie. This turned out to be the legal ground that needed to be reclaimed; and, as soon as he did that, he experienced a tremendous sense of freedom. Breaking the soul tie had loosed him from bondage.

Evicting. Not only is authority used for binding and loosing, but authority is also used to evict wicked spirits. In the New Testament we frequently see Jesus or one of the apostles casting out demons with a simple declaration of authority, and it can create the idea that this is always how it is done. As hundreds of people can testify, however, there are many occasions when a simple command of authority in the name of Jesus does no good, because the demon has legal ground that needs to be removed. The exception to this seems to be what some have called "power encounters." A power encounter occurs when there is a contest between the power of Satan and the power of Christ.

Elijah had a power encounter with the prophets of Baal on Mt. Carmel. Many missionaries have power encounters with witchdoctors or pagan priests in the areas where they serve. If missionaries are not equipped for such encounters, it can be disastrous.

In one African village the missionary was called into a hut to pray for a man who had been shot. He came in and looked around but determined that this man needed medicine and surgery, not prayer. He said some sort of standard, pastoral prayer for the man, but then left to make medical arrangements. While he was gone, the family called in the witchdoctor. He went through a ritual and began dancing around the man and chanting. Suddenly, the bullet levitated from the man's arm, and the shaman snatched it out of the air with his hand. Now, how much chance do you think that missionary was going to have of convincing those people that Jesus was the true God?

By way of contrast, there are many stories of missionaries who have overcome the power of witchcraft through the power of our risen Savior. One powerful witchdoctor credited with killing hundreds of people with her sorcery converted almost immediately when a curse she placed on a missionary failed to kill him. The missionary was riding his bike down a path in the jungle when a fireball appeared out of nowhere and destroyed his bike. Undeterred, the brave Christian continued on foot to the village and presented himself to the tribal witchdoctor. The demonstration of Christ's power in protecting the missionary paved the way for many in that village to give their lives to Christ, beginning with the witchdoctor herself.[2] In another power encounter, a group of Muslims in North Africa approached the Christians in the community to join them in asking God for

---

2 | The full story is Loren Entz, "Challenge to Abou's Jesus," In *Evangelical Missions Quarterly* 22 (January 1986). p. 49. Cited in Timothy M. Warner, *Spiritual Warfare* (Wheaton: Crossway, 1991) pp. 129-130.

drought-ending rain. The Christians said no. Instead, they told the Muslims to pick a date and time to pray for rain and they would pray separately on a different day. The Muslim day of prayer came and went without a cloud in the sky. When the Christians gathered it immediately became overcast. Many Muslim leaders came out and began to pray, but the clouds went away. They apologized and asked the Christians to pray again. Within an hour, there was a downpour. Many people gave their lives to Christ in that village.

Evictions as power encounters such as we see in the Gospels seem to serve an evangelistic function. They establish the credibility of the message. In fact, I was recently told of a secret gathering of leaders from a country that persecutes Christians in which they were discussing a theological conundrum. They were trying to understand why they were able to heal people so routinely in evangelistic settings but that prayers for the sick after conversion did not seem to be as effective. In a way, the very fact that this experience was so wide-spread and universal seems to point to the conclusion that such miracles and demonic evictions were used by God as power encounters to confirm the truth of the Gospel.[3]

Within the Christian community, however, evictions most commonly follow the reclaiming of surrendered ground. Many times, when a Christian confesses sin and forgives those who have wronged him, no eviction is necessary. The reclaiming of the ground leads immediately to a release from the enemy's activity. But there are other times, especially if the legal ground is related to the occult, violence, or has been there for a long time, perhaps even for generations, that an eviction will need to follow. One way to test this is to simply pray, using the word **if**. "Lord, *if* the enemy has claimed a right to harass me because of this sin, then in the

---

3 | For more on power encounters, see the chapter "The Christian on the Offensive" in Timothy M. Warner's book *Spiritual Warfare*.

name of Jesus, I command him to leave and go where the Lord Jesus sends him."

Sometimes it is obvious there is still a demonic presence because the demon is actively interfering or manifesting. Sometimes this can be dealt with quickly, but at times there is more legal ground that needs to be removed. At times like this it can be helpful to use a standardized prayer that covers most of the common ways in which demons gain legal ground in a person's life. Dr. Mark Bubeck often uses something called "The Round Up" prayer for this purpose.[4]

It is also a good idea to simply pray, "Lord Jesus, will You please show us if we have missed anything?" and let the Holy Spirit guide you to the missing ground. Sometimes the missing ingredient is simply the person's confidence. The demon is waiting to see if the person doing the evicting really believes. I have seen more than one demon flee after a person who had been victimized and reduced to slavery for years finally began to affirm their true identity in Christ and, often for the first time in their lives, stand up to the demons and fight for what was theirs.

Discussion Questions

1. In what way is authority different than power?

2. What is wrong with the idea that Christians have NO authority?

3. What is wrong with the idea that Christians have ALL authority?

---

[4] | See Appendix 3.

4. What does it mean to have limited authority?

5. What stood out to you about the three uses of authority described in this chapter?

6. What takeaways did you get from this chapter?

Personal Exercise

The next time you read your Bible and pray, say the following prayer first.

"In the name of Jesus, I bind any demons that have been assigned to hinder my ability to read or understand the Bible. I also bind any demons assigned to hinder my prayers. I ask, instead, that the Holy Spirit would open the eyes of my heart to what He wants me to see and speak to me during my time of prayer."

Bible Study

Here are some of the Bible passages referenced in this chapter. Read through each of them and write down any observations you have.[5]

- Philippians 2:7-11 – . . . he emptied himself, taking the form of a slave and being made in the likeness of mankind. Being found in appearance as a man, he humbled himself by becoming obedient to the point of death, even death on a cross. Therefore,

---
5 | Author's translation.

God exalted [Jesus] and **granted him a name that is above every name,** that at the name of Jesus every knee should bow in heaven and on earth and under the earth, and every language acknowledge that Jesus Christ is Lord to the glory of God the Father.

- Matthew 28:18-20 – Jesus came to them and said, **"All authority in heaven and on earth has been given to me.** Therefore, as you go, disciple every ethnic group, baptizing them into the name of the Father, the Son, and the Holy Spirit, and teach them to keep everything I have commanded you. And behold, I am with you always until the end of the age."

- Revelation 12:4a – [The great red dragon's] tail swept down a third of the stars of heaven and cast them to earth. *(Stars are likely a metaphor for angels.)*

- Psalm 8:5 – You have made [man] a little lower than the gods *(Hebrew text)* or angels *(Septuagint text)* and crowned him with glory and honor.

- Ephesians 2:5-6 – [God] made us alive together with Christ . . . and raised us up with him and seated us with him in the heavenly realms in Christ Jesus.

Four
The Process

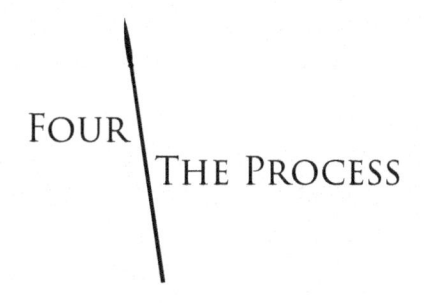

I remember the first time someone came to see me with the anticipation that I could help them find freedom from the demonic torment they were experiencing. I was scared to death. I wasn't so much afraid of the demons as I was of disappointing the person. One of the lessons I had to learn early on was that I am no one's savior. As many others have discovered, there is only one Wonderful Counselor—only one Messiah—and it isn't me or you.

In the last two chapters we explored the two core principles at the heart of spiritual warfare ministry: permission and authority. In this chapter we will look at how to reclaim surrendered ground and use our delegated authority to find freedom from spiritual bondage. I will use two memory devices to a give structure to this chapter.

The first one comes from Dr. Karl Payne. It is CCC: Confess, Cancel, and Command. This is a simple pattern that helps people remember the essential elements of evicting an evil spirit. We have added the word "Commit." Karl also teaches the concept of this step, but we added it here to the usual three C's he teaches as an official fourth C.

The second memory device is SOUL-L: sin, occult, unforgiveness, lies we believe, and lineage. This is a list of the five most common doorways that give legal ground to the enemy. Most of the legal ground that will have to be reclaimed from the enemy relates to one of these five areas.

CCC-C

Karl Payne uses a simple three-step process for evicting demonic spirits that is easy to remember. It is the three Cs: Confess, Cancel, and Command. First, you confess the sin; then you cancel any claim the demons may have based on that sin; and then you command the demons to leave. When demons know that they have no more legal ground, and when they know that you know they have no more legal ground, it is usually not difficult to make them leave. The problems tend to arise when you don't remove the legal ground.

- **Confess:** I confess that I _____ (believed lies, sinned, participated in the occult, engaged in a specific activity that needs to be renounced).
- **Cancel:** I ask Jesus to cancel any claim that any demon may have against me in the courtroom of heaven.
- **Command:** In the name of the Lord Jesus Christ, I command every wicked spirit who has been assigned to me to leave, go where the Lord Jesus sends you, and take all of your works and effects with you.
- **Commit:** I commit this area of my life to Jesus Christ. I ask Him to cleanse me, fill me with His Spirit, and occupy the place the demons have left.

SOUL-L

Earlier I introduced five doorways that give the devil a place in our lives: Sin, the Occult, Unforgiveness, Lies we believe, and Lineage. Each of these issues has a remedy. The remedy for sin is repentance. The remedy for the occult is renunciation. The remedy for unforgiveness is forgiveness. The remedy for lies is replacing them with the truth. The remedy for sins that come to us through our family line is to cut off the demonic access.

Neil Anderson's *Steps to Freedom in Christ* is a comprehensive inventory of the seven most common areas in which we surrender legal ground to the devil (occult, deception, bitterness, pride, rebellion, habitual sin, and generational sin). It is an excellent tool for walking yourself or someone else through the renunciations and prayers most commonly required to reclaim surrendered ground.

Sin. Ephesians 4:26-27 says that sin gives the devil a foothold in your life. To reclaim ground surrendered to the enemy through sin, we simply have to confess that sin. If a demon did enter a person on the basis of the legal ground given by that sin, confession cancels the demon's claim. That does not mean, however, that the demon automatically leaves. Demons often have to be evicted. It is no different than sending a notice to a renter who refuses to pay their lease that they have been evicted and sending the police to enforce the notice and forcibly evict the squatters. Confession is like going to the courtroom of heaven to get the eviction notice. It cancels their legal claim to a place in your life. But sometimes you have to call in the police. You do this by actively addressing the demons and commanding them to leave in the name of Jesus. Sometimes I have even asked Jesus to send holy angels to escort them out. (I don't command holy angels to do anything. It doesn't seem appropriate. But I often ask Jesus for angelic support!)

A sample prayer for confessing and canceling legal ground:

"In the name of Jesus, I confess my participation in _____. I renounce my participation in this sin and hereby cancel the ground in my life claimed by my enemy. In the name of Jesus, I now command every demon who took advantage of this ground to renounce their claim on me and leave. You must go where the Lord Jesus sends you."

Occult. If sin opens the door to the devil, then the occult is like opening a garage door. It is sin that puts you directly into contact with the demonic. In the next chapter I am going to explain this area more fully. For now, I just want to explain how to find freedom from occult involvement.

Ending Satan's claim on your life because of occult activity begins with the three C's. You must confess that you did it, cancel any claim the enemy may have on you, and command the demons to leave. It is sometimes also necessary to destroy the occult objects you own or that have been used to grant them access to your world.

One tribal priest whose family had served a pagan god in Africa for ten generations made a decisive break with his occult background. He gave his life to Christ and got baptized, then went to the ritual site where the idol was located. He announced to the spirit that he would no longer serve him. He destroyed the idol and burned it in a fire, then for good measure he sprayed his own urine all over the "sacred" site. Now, that is what I would call a full renunciation of one's occult involvement!

Unforgiveness. The obvious antidote to unforgiveness is forgiveness. There are a few principles about forgiveness, however, that are worth mentioning. First, forgiveness is a choice not a feeling. When you forgive someone, you are canceling the debt that is owed to you. In this sense, it is a business transaction. You might picture yourself in front of a judge who is asking you, "Are you going to cancel the debt or not?" Your emotions don't really enter into it from a legal perspective.

However, the Bible tells us to forgive others "from the heart." This does not mean that we have to wait to choose to forgive them until we feel like forgiving them. It means that we need to get in touch with our feelings when we forgive and not simply say the words out of obligation. God does not want us to simply go through the motions, nor does He want us to simply pretend everything is okay. He wants us to trust Him to take care of us and to leave the debt and the right to vengeance in His hands.

Another important principle about forgiveness is that it isn't the same as reconciliation. Reconciliation takes two. Forgiveness only takes one. You can cancel a debt without the other person being in the courtroom. Reconciliation, however, is the reestablishment of a relationship and the rebuilding of trust. Without forgiveness, reconciliation will not be possible, but forgiveness alone does not produce reconciliation.

This was driven home to me by the story of a pastor who was called to a home where the wife had just found out that her husband had been cheating on her with a close friend. All sorts of scenarios ran through this pastor's mind of what he would find when he arrived. What he found, however, was nothing like what he had expected.

When he arrived, the husband was angry with the wife, rather than the other way around! The husband was angry because his wife would not "forgive" him. The man told the pastor, "Tell my wife she needs to forgive me. Tell her she needs to give me a kiss, put this behind us, and go on like it never happened." This husband actually believed this would be the biblical thing to do! The reality is that he was confusing forgiveness with reconciliation, and in the process was trying to absolve himself of any consequences for what he had done.

Forgiveness does not mean there will be no consequences. I can forgive my child for rebellion against me. It doesn't mean there won't be a time out or worse. The discipline is part of the restoration process. There are times when mercy will reduce punishment or even remove it, but this is not required by forgiveness.

When it comes to the process of forgiving, I encourage people to take the following steps:

1. Ask God to help you think about the person in the way in which they are the most offensive to you. This helps you get your heart engaged, so that you can forgive from your heart.

2. Reflect on the negative emotions and negative consequences you have had to bear because of what the other person has done.

3. Make a declaration: "In the name of Jesus, I choose to forgive ___ for . . ." and list the wrong behavior and negative consequences imposed against you.

4. Ask Jesus to help you think about the person in the way in which He wants you to think about them. Ask Him to help you understand why He loves that person, so that you can learn to love them, too.

5. Pray a blessing on the person you forgave and ask the Lord to bring them what is good (even if that good thing is repentance that leads to life).

Lies we believe. The devil is the "father of lies" (John 8:44). When we believe his lies rather than God's truth it is like shaking hands with the devil and saying, "You are right, and God is wrong. I agree with you." Our agreement with his narrative gives him permission to a place in our lives. One of the most common ways this happens is through the lies we learn from pain in our past. In the book *Understanding the Wounded Heart*, I describe a common pattern in which the devil succeeds in planting his lies in wounded places in our hearts. The model can be remembered as WLVS:

Wounds

Lies

Vows

Strongholds

Wounds create fertile soil in which the devil plants lies about God, about who we are, and about how life works. Our flesh responds to these lies by making vows about how we will take control of this area of our lives. Such vows are usually "I will" statements in which we say something like, "I will never let this happen again." Because we no longer trust God with this painful area in our lives, our flesh takes over. The result is a stronghold in which the world, the devil, and the flesh work together to keep us in bondage.

Not all lies are rooted in wounds. Sometimes we believe lies because of comparison or because of misperceptions or because someone suggests a lie that feels true to us. Whatever the source, agreeing with the enemy's lies gives him permission to a place in our lives.

One helpful approach for resolving the problem of lies we believe is to ask Jesus to show us if there are beliefs and narratives controlling our emotions and behavior that are not from Him. As an exercise, write down the thoughts that come to mind, even if they feel like they are true or factual. Then, ask Jesus to show you His truth. Next, pray a simple prayer where you break agreement with the lies and choose to believe the truth God has shown you.

Lineage. In Western culture, we do not often think about the impact of prior generations on our lives in the present. We are so individualistic that we forget our lives flow out of a source (like our family tree), which often has impurities in it that affect us.

Demons from past generations can affect people in the present. Perhaps great grandpa murdered someone, or grandma practiced witchcraft, or dad developed a porn addiction and committed adultery. Any of these sins would open a door into that person's family tree. As a consequence, those demons will have greater access to the members of that family than if the door had not been opened. If you are born into a family that has already opened the door to demonic activity, it is going to affect you. Once demons gain ground in a family, they are going to look for ways to stay, and they are going to seek to extend their claims to the next generation.

One young man who scheduled an appointment because of frequent panic attacks was surprised to learn there was an ancestral element to his problem. During our time together, he asked God to show him the original event that had opened the door to fear in his life. He remembered being alone in a bathroom when he was about seven years old and feeling like something jumped on his back. He was terrified and had his first panic attack.

When I asked him if any other family members struggled with fear or high levels of worry, he mentioned that both his mother and grandmother were consumed with worry. We decided it was best to renounce any ancestral sin that may have opened a door to the demonic in his family line. As I led him through the prayer, he got stuck. He couldn't finish saying the word "Jesus." Only half of the word would come out no matter how hard he focused. He was getting interference from a demon. We bound the wicked spirit, finished the prayer, and evicted the spirit involved. Afterward, the young man said, "I never would have dreamed that my problems had roots in my family line."

A couple who adopted a child from a Muslim background had no end of behavioral problems with him. People frequently referred to him as a "holy terror," and he was regularly in trouble at school. They were at their wits' end on how to deal with him, when someone suggested they cut off any wicked spirits that may have come with him from his ancestral background. One night, while the boy was sleeping, his parents prayed over him and canceled any claim the enemy had on their adopted son because of the sins of his ancestors, and they commanded those spirits to leave in the name of Jesus. In the middle of the prayer the boy flopped out of his bed. He woke up and asked what had happened. His parents reassured him that everything was okay, and he went back to sleep. The next morning, they could already notice a difference in the level of calmness in the child. By the end of the week his teacher sent home a note saying, "I don't know what you've been doing with your son, but whatever it is, keep it up!" Dealing with the spirits that had come down through the family line did not make the boy perfect, but they did remove a major obstacle to his development.

Dealing with generational sin follows the same four-C pattern as before. Confess the sin that gave the ground. In this case it is the sin of an ancestor. You can confess all sins generally that have given ground whether you know about the sin or not, but it is a good idea to list the ones of which you are specifically aware, especially if they were habitual or traumatic. Cancel the ground claimed by the enemy because of that sin. Specifically cancel any claim they may have on future generations. Command the demons to leave. Commit the person to Christ's care.

Cleansing Property. Just as demons can claim a legal right to a person because of unresolved sin, they can claim a legal right to a piece of property, access to an institution (like a school or a church), or ownership of an object (especially one created or dedicated for occult purposes like an amulet or an idol). Land that has been polluted by sin must be redeemed before it can be used for God's glory.

For example, when Nehemiah returned for his second term as governor and found that one of his officers had allowed a pagan official to move into a room of the temple; Nehemiah not only evicted the pagan official, he discarded all of his things (13:7-8). One can only assume that this man had been practicing his pagan religion in that room of the temple.

Cleansing property is often as simple as renouncing what may have taken place there in the past and inviting Jesus to fill the place with His presence. I know of situations in which someone moved into a home where occult rituals had been held in the basement. They experienced paranormal activity in the house (doors slamming, objects floating, ghosts appearing, etc.) before they discovered that someone had painted over several Satanic symbols on the basement walls and realized that this activity had never been renounced and that the spirits had never been made to leave. They did so, and the paranormal activity stopped.

This same principle implies that any objects that have been devoted to pagan or satanic use need to be destroyed. This can be especially difficult when the object is considered a family heirloom or of great cultural significance. This can also be taken to an extreme, and discernment is called for. My basic rule of thumb is that if an object was created for and used for an occult purpose (e.g., a Masonic ritual or pagan worship), then I destroy it. If it is an ordinary object, but I suspect that someone has placed a curse on it, I simply "cleanse" it and command the spirit attached to it to leave.

Taking Thoughts Captive. In order to live in freedom, it is not enough to get rid of demons, we also have to stay free of demons. One of the most effective ways of doing this is to develop the practice of taking your thoughts captive. The principle here is that not every thought that enters your head is yours.

My dad tells the story of a professor in a theological school who came to see him because he was troubled by the perverted sexual thoughts that often came to his mind when he began to pray. He was afraid that he had a demon and needed a "deliverance session." After a little probing, however, my dad realized that this man had not surrendered any legal ground that would give the demons a right to this type of oppression.

The man asked him, "What's wrong with me?"

My dad replied, "There is probably nothing wrong with you. There is probably something right about you, and that is why the enemy is trying to convince you that you shouldn't be in ministry. If you haven't put those perverted thoughts in your mind, and you can be sure God isn't doing that, where do you think they come from?" Instead of casting out a "demon of perversion," my dad taught him how to take his thoughts captive.

About a year later, they saw each other again and the man said, "I just want to thank you for meeting with me last year. When I first came, I thought you might pray over me and get rid of a demon, but I'm really glad it didn't happen like that. Learning how to take my thoughts captive has changed me, changed my family, and I am returning to my ministry in Africa with a whole new perspective on it." Like this ministry leader, most of us have no idea how much junk we let go unchallenged in our thinking because we assume the thoughts are just ours.

Taking thoughts captive is not difficult. It is an intentional choice to reject a message from the enemy and replace it with the truth, or to expose the enemy and command him to leave. Recognizing the need to do this and choosing to do it can be difficult. Demonic thoughts often challenge God's truth. For example, God loves you and you are precious to Him. But how many thoughts do you have on a daily basis that attempt to rob you of the joy of that truth—thoughts that you are a disappointment to God or that He is disgusted with you or that He cannot be trusted to have your best interest at heart? Such thoughts do not come from God. They are temptations of the Enemy intended to rob you of intimacy with God. Recognizing, resisting, and replacing these thoughts is the essence of taking them captive.

A good way to practice taking your thoughts captive (and to demonstrate the reality of spiritual warfare) is to try to keep this thought in the forefront of your thinking all day:

"I am the apple of God's eye. His love for me is so vast it cannot be measured."

As you do this, pay attention to the contrary thoughts that try to rob you of the joy of these truths. At some point, command any demons that are telling you those lies to leave. Then ask the Lord to confirm His truth to you in a fresh way!

Conclusion

The process of identifying and evicting demonic spirits is not a magical formula based on using the right words. It is primarily about making sure that the legal ground giving permission to the enemy is removed and then specifically commanding the enemy to leave.

A good tool for going through this process is *The Steps to Freedom in Christ* by Neil T. Anderson.

Discussion Questions

1. Do you remember what CCC-C stands for?

2. Do you remember what SOUL-L stands for?

3. Have you ever experienced a sense of freedom after forgiving, repenting, or renouncing something the devil was using against you?

4. Can you think of a time when taking thoughts captive helped you? Can you think of a time when it would have helped?

Personal Exercise

First, use the SOUL-L paradigm to do a personal inventory of areas in your life in which you may have surrendered ground to the enemy. Then for each of these areas go through the CCC-C process of confessing, canceling, commanding, and committing.

Sin: Father in heaven, please bring to my mind any sin in my life which the enemy is using to claim permission to a place in my life. *(rebellion, idolatry, pride, sexual immorality, etc.)*

Occult: "Father in heaven, please bring to my mind any way in which I have opened a door to the enemy through occult participation." *(astrology, fortune telling, Ouija boards, spells, curses, etc.)*

Unforgiveness: "Please bring to my mind the names of people I need to forgive."

I choose to forgive _____ for _____ and for making me feel _____. I ask you to cancel any permission my bitterness has given the enemy to a place in my life. In the name of the Lord Jesus Christ, I command all demons related to bitterness to leave and take all of their works and effects with them.

Lies we believe: "If I have believed a lie that has undermined my freedom, please bring that lie to mind." *(Write it out. Renounce it and cancel any permission the enemy may claim because of it. Invite Jesus to give you a new perspective and write that down.)*

Lineage: Draw out a simple family tree as far back as you can remember. Ask God to remind you of any known sins in your ancestry that were unresolved. On behalf of your family, renounce those sins, cancel the permission they give to demonic activity in your family line, and command the demons to leave and take all of their works and effects with them. Close by committing your family to Christ's protection.

FIVE
DEMONS AND DECEPTION

Years ago, I met with a young lady who had been diagnosed with schizophrenia. She was hearing voices that were telling her to hurt members of her family. Sometimes the radio or the television would deliver secret messages just for her. Now, there is a physical problem that can affect the brain and cause genuine schizophrenia, but that was not this girl's problem. The psychological community simply had no other diagnosis for what she was experiencing. She met with me to go through the *Steps to Freedom*. One of the first questions I asked her was whether she had ever participated in the occult. She said no. I was skeptical. Symptoms like hers usually implied some form of occult engagement.

When I pulled out the list of occult activities found in the *Steps to Freedom* and began to explain them to her, she circled half the list! She had gone through mind control seminars where you learn to read someone else's thoughts. She had practiced levitation, participated in séances, used Ouija boards, and played with tarot cards. You name it, it seemed like she had done it. She just didn't know there was anything wrong with this stuff. On top of this, she had been living with her boyfriend; so, she had baggage from sexual sin. And to make matters worse, her boyfriend was an occultist who put a curse on her when she left him!

Over the course of two sessions, I was able to walk her through prayers of renunciation and eviction. She renounced her sexual sin and broke soul ties with her boyfriend. She also broke the curse that had been placed on her. Along the way I helped her understand her identity in Christ and her position of victory over the enemy. By the time we were done, she wasn't hearing voices anymore. Stories like this remind us of the dangers of the occult and the freedom that can be found in Christ.

Demons

Within the spirit realm are many creatures. The Bible talks about the sons of God (Job 1:6), watchers (Daniel 4:17), a divine council (Psalm 82:1), thrones (Daniel 7:9; Colossians 1:16; Revelation 4:4; 11:16; 20:4), cherubim (Genesis 3:24, etc.), seraphim (Isaiah 6:2,6), messenger angels (Zechariah 1:9, etc.), principalities (Ephesians 3:10, etc.), powers (Romans 8:38; Ephesians 6:12), and more. Our primary concern here is not with the higher-ranking spirits that relate to world affairs, but with the lower-level evil spirits (demons) that torment people.

The most common Greek word for demon is *daimonion* from the core Greek word *daimon*. As you can see, our English versions didn't really translate the word, they just borrowed it. In the New Testament, a *daimon* or *daimonion* was any malevolent spirit that oppressed you or made life difficult for you. The words are never explained. It is assumed the readers know what they are. When they took control of a person, they could affect their bodies, minds, and emotions. There are two major theories about demonic origins.

Theory #1 is that demons are fallen angels. This theory gained great popularity because of John Milton's epic novel *Paradise Lost*,[1] which describes Lucifer's fall in great detail. Most evangelicals have been taught that Satan rebelled out of pride (Isaiah 14 and Ezekiel 28) and took a third of the angels with him (Revelation 12:5) when he fell like lightning from heaven (Luke 10:18). In speculating as to why Satan

---

[1] | The complete text of *Paradise Lost* can be read online at https://archive.org/stream/ParadiseLost1674#page/n4/mode/1up

rebelled, Milton put these words in his mouth, "Better to reign in hell than serve in heaven."[2] I was taught this view, and for years it was the only theory I knew. However, there is another theory that deserves exploration.

Theory #2 dates back to the intertestamental period and can be found in the Dead Sea Scrolls and the Book of Enoch. It has recently been popularized by Dr. Michael Heiser, an Old Testament scholar who has written several popular books on the spirit world.[3] This theory states that demons are the disembodied spirits of the Nephilim mentioned in Genesis 6 as the offspring of the "sons of God" and the "daughters of men." The Book of Enoch refers to the sons of God as "Watchers" (this term is also used in Daniel 4:13, 23). This writing goes into great detail about the Genesis 6 event which it interprets as a violation of the boundary God established between heavenly beings and earthly beings. As part of God's judgment, He consigns the spirits of the demigod hybrids to roam the earth.

> And now, the giants [Nephilim] who were born from body and flesh will be called Evil Spirits on the Earth, and on the Earth will be their dwelling. And evil spirits came out from their flesh, because from above they were created, from the Holy Watchers was their origin and first foundation. Evil spirits they will be on Earth and 'Spirits of the Evil Ones' they will be called (15:8-9).

This second theory recognizes two classes of wicked spirits, heavenly beings who rebelled (fallen angels) and the spirits of the Nephilim. Whether you embrace theory one

---

[2] | *Paradise Lost* (1674) p. 13 – Literal wording: "Better to reign in Hell then serve in Heav'n." https://archive.org/stream/ParadiseLost1674#page/n13/mode/1up/search/reign+in+hell

[3] | Dr. Heiser's books include: *The Unseen Realm, Reversing Hermon, Angels, Demons,* and more.

or theory two doesn't really affect the practice of spiritual warfare. Either way, demons are subject to the authority of those who are in Christ. The origin story—while interesting to study—does not change our approach to helping people find freedom from demonic torment.

While we are exploring the identity of demons, it is worth noting that the Bible refers to the gods of the nations as demons (Deuteronomy 32:16-17; Psalm 106:37; 1 Corinthians 10:20-22). These texts suggest there are high-ranking fallen angels (principalities and powers) that are worshiped as gods.

There are millions of gods and lesser supernatural beings in this world, and all of them want some level of power over humans. It may be that Satan enticed some of his fellow angels to follow him by promising them that they would be gods. It does not take much imagination to hear him ask the other angels, "Do you want to serve the humans, or do you want the humans to serve you?" It would seem that every demon wants power over humans. They accomplish this by seeking to make slaves out of people to the fullest extent possible.

Demons can rule over regions, institutions, and people.

Paul often referred to principalities and powers (Romans 8:38; Ephesians 3:10; 6:12; Colossians 1:16; 2:15; Titus 3:1). The term "principality" implies one who rules over a region. The Greek word is *arche* (pronounced: ar-kay'). It is often used of earthly leaders and can be translated *head* or *ruler*. One of the reasons God is so opposed to idolatry is that nations that serve false gods are entering into a pact with a high-ranking demon and all of the demons beneath it in rank who serve it. This pact gives those demons a right to greater power and activity in that region.

This is why some countries or territories have much more overt demonic activity than others. Wicked spirits have been invited in and given authority by the earthly rulers of the region. You can see this principle at work in countries like Haiti where, after they had expelled their French overlords, the leaders dedicated their nation to the devil in a well-known voodoo ceremony—a ceremony repeated in 1992. You can also see it in regions where annual rituals renew that territory's dedication to a false god.[4] I spoke to one tribal king who described the annual ritual in which he participated to summon the demon-god of their people to appear. Each year, the tribal leaders went through a ritual in which the waters of a lake were troubled, and a spirit would appear and speak to them. The tribe would declare their allegiance to this spirit thereby giving it permission to rule in their territory.

Demons can exercise power over nature.

Not only did Paul often refer to demons as principalities, he also used the word "powers." The word is *exousia* (ex-oo-see'-ah) and is probably better translated "authorities." Such demons have authority in the realm of nature and the ability to cause natural phenomenon.

Most of the gods of paganism are nature gods, who are able to exercise a certain amount of control over the forces of nature. According to Canaanite mythology, Baal had the ability to send rain and cause storms. His priests were probably shocked when Baal was unable to send fire from the sky in their contest with Elijah (1 Kings 18:20-29). If they knew there was no chance Baal could do it, they never would have agreed to the contest.

---

4 | George Otis and the Sentinel Group have produced several excellent videos called "Transformations." These and Dr. Otis's book *Twilight Labyrinth* provide an in-depth look at the idea of territorial spirits. For a good academic study of principalities and powers, see Dr. Clinton Arnold's book *Three Crucial Questions* (Grand Rapids: Baker Academic 1997).

In a similar way, the magi of Egypt were able to turn a staff into a snake and water into blood through their magic arts (Exodus 7:11, 22; 8:7, 18). We also see in Revelation that angels are able to hold back the wind (7:1) and impact nature from the unseen realm as we see when they pour out bowls of wrath that do great damage to the natural realm (Revelation 16). In stories like these, the Bible recognizes that demons (and angels) have a certain amount of power over nature.

Deception

If I were going to summarize the enemy's work in one sentence, it would be this: *demons lay snares.* Demons use deception to lure individuals (and often entire communities) into choices that will bring them and their offspring into bondage. Ultimately, he wants to destroy them. This is why the Bible urges us to avoid those activities that will bring us under the enemy's control and to repent in order to break free from enemy snares.

A common strategy for ensnaring a family, church, culture, or other group is to introduce competing narratives to create division. I have been told that some enemies of the gospel intentionally infiltrate churches by sending two people with the specific agenda of causing a split. They are often quickly accepted because they give of their time, donate money, and quote Scripture freely. Each will befriend a different church leader and gradually encourage them to adopt a narrative of distrust about each other. Neither person grabs the spotlight, but the narratives they spin create division and each leader gathers people around them that they trust. Soon there are two camps in the church, and, before long, a split occurs.

Whenever you see division, you also see deception. This is heightened when you add narcissistic leadership into the mix that refuses to take blame and silences those who disagree.

In order to understand deception, you can think of it as a magic trick. When an illusionist saws his assistant in half, we know that isn't actually happening, but it looks like it. The trick is to get us to focus on only those true observations that lead to the conclusion that magic has happened. The illusionist hides from us the fact that there are two ladies in two boxes. One lady has her head showing, the other is showing her feet. It is the truth he hides from us that creates the illusion.

In the same way, the devil tries to hide truth that would change our narrative. By getting us to focus only on certain true things and ignoring others, he can get us to believe a narrative that allows him to control our lives. For example, I may feel like a worthless person because I can point to several times in my life when I have done bad things or people have told me I was worthless. As long as I only review those facts that support the narrative, I see no way that my conclusion can be wrong. However, if a few new facts were introduced, it might change everything. Just like knowing there is a second lady in a second box changes your whole outlook on the magic trick.

The devil is the father of lies (John 8:44). Consequently, wherever you find deception, you find the work of the devil. The demonic work of deception can be divided into three parts: thoughts, tapes, and voices.

Thoughts. Not every thought that enters your head is yours. Some come from the Holy Spirit. They give you guidance and encouragement. Some come from demons. They tempt you to fear and unbelief. You can think of the demonic attack on your thoughts as the "fiery darts" mentioned in Ephesians 6:16. Satan shoots his flaming arrows at you in the form of tempting thoughts. The proper response to these is to hold up the shield of faith in order to resist them and then to counterattack with the Sword of the Spirit, which is the Word of God. This process is commonly called "taking your thoughts captive" (2 Corinthians 10:5). Martin Luther is credited for saying, "You can't keep a bird from landing on your head, but you can keep him from building a nest there." In a sense, that is what we do when we resist the enemy. We are keeping the devil from building a nest in our thought life.

Tapes. Sometimes the devil succeeds in planting thoughts in our hearts that develop into "tapes" that play over and over. These are deceptive patterns of thinking that keep us from living in the freedom of who we really are. These tapes are usually lies that target who we are, who God is, and how life works. For example, sometimes these tapes take the form of persistent negative thoughts about family members, friends, or even ministry associates. Such thought patterns can be debilitating to our marriage, our parenting, and our other relationships.

Above all, the enemy targets our view of God and our view of ourselves. If Satan is a roaring lion looking to eat a sheep, what is that sheep's best defense? It is to stay close to the Shepherd. Sometimes we get the idea that our job is to become "super sheep" so that we can take on the devil in our own strength. But Satan knows that our defense lies in staying close to the Shepherd. He knows that if he is going to have a good lunch, he needs to lure us away from the Shepherd, and his primary tactic for doing this is deception. If he can get you to believe that you are such a bad sheep that the Shepherd is disgusted with you, there is a good chance you are going to avoid the Shepherd. Or, if he can convince you that the Shepherd is not completely trustworthy, if he can point out reasons to be disappointed with the Shepherd, he knows you are less likely to stay close to him. Therefore, Satan's primary objective is to fill your mind with lies about yourself and about God that will keep you isolated from Him. The result is that most of us spend our lives trying to perform for God and earn His acceptance, rather than enjoying His presence. Our isolation makes us much easier prey for the enemy.

The most common way that tapes form in our minds is through trauma. When our hearts are broken by suffering, the physical and/or emotional wounds create fertile soil into which Satan is able to plant the seeds of deception. If these lies feel true to us, we will enter into an agreement with the devil and accept them as true. When this happens, the lies take root in our hearts and begin to grow. We begin to make decisions about how we will live our lives as if these lies are true. These vows we make are like vines that begin to bear fruit. However, it is not the fruit of the Spirit that is produced but the fruit of deception. These lies in our hearts produce fear, depression, shame, disgust, anger, and hopelessness.

Replacing these tapes in our heads requires a renewal of the mind. It may also require a healing of the heart. We will need to go back to the original wounds into which the devil planted his lies in order to pull this vine out by the roots.

Voices. Some people hear voices in their heads. This does not mean they are crazy. Voices in the head can be demons. This is normally a sign that the person has either been involved in the occult or has been the victim of abuse.

Voices in the head can also be other "parts" or "personalities." People who have experienced extreme trauma often dissociate and form alternate personalities. Usually, one or more parts are protectors (also called guardians), one or more parts keep the pain in secrecy and isolation, and there are sometimes other parts who have other jobs. These parts were formed in the brain as a means of self-preservation. They often function as completely different individuals; though, they are actually different parts of the same core person. Sometimes the different parts of them talk to each other inside, and this can cause the experience of voices in the head.[5]

If the voices are demonic, they can be removed by using the three C's: confess, cancel, and command. I was recently speaking on spiritual warfare at a church and describing the characteristics of a demonized person. I mentioned that sometimes they hear voices in their heads, and a woman spoke up: "I hear voices in my head. And I see a demon following me around." She went on to say that her psychologist said she was schizophrenic and didn't believe that it was really a demon that was harassing her.

After my presentation, we prayed together. She renounced the legal ground in her life and commanded the demons to leave. She also prayed and cancelled any claim on her children that the demons might have through her sin or through the generational sin in her family.

The next week, when I returned for part two of my series, she asked if she could share her testimony with the class. In the past week she had not heard a single voice in her head, and the demon had disappeared. Life in her home had also become much calmer. Best of all, her teenage son had prayed to receive Christ! Needless to say, results aren't always that dramatic, but it is instructive to understand just how life-changing it can be to know and apply the principles of spiritual warfare.

Deceptive Power

Demonic activity is always rooted in deception. This does not mean demons do not have real power or that this power does not often appear to help people. It means they use their power to deceive. Many miracles have been done in the name of Jesus that were performed by the power of the occult and

---

[5] | For more on dissociation see *A D.I.D. Primer*, by Marcus Warner.

had nothing to do with the true Jesus, who was born of a virgin, crucified, and raised as Lord of all.

I know of a man in full-time Christian ministry who had a withered leg. He went to a faith healer who laid hands on him, and the leg miraculously straightened. After that experience, however, he began to slip into a depression that was threatening to run him out of ministry and into an institution.

At the advice of an experienced pastor, he tested the healing with something we call "an **If** Prayer." It went something like this: "If this healing came from God, I give Him thanks and glory, but if I have been deceived and this healing is from the devil, then, in the name of Jesus, I renounce it now and command the demon involved to leave." Immediately, his leg returned to the way it had been, and his depression left.

Many people get lured into the New Age, occult activity, and counterfeit religion through experiences of power.

Discussion Questions

1. Why do you think it is important for Christians to understand demons?

2. What did you learn about demons in this chapter? How was this helpful?

3. How would you explain the power of deception?

4. Have you ever had thoughts, tapes, or voices create problems for you? If you found freedom from these, what did you find helpful?

Personal Exercise

This journaling exercise has two parts. First, pick one of the suggested issues listed below and ask God to show you what words and images the devil has been using to deceive you. Write out the words and picture that come to mind. Second, ask God to give you new words or pictures that come from Him that show you the truth He wants you to believe.

Father in heaven, please show me in words or pictures how Satan has been trying to deceive me about . . .

- Myself
- You
- My spouse
- A specific situation

Father in heaven, please show me in words or pictures the new thoughts You want me to have about this issue.

Six
The Occult

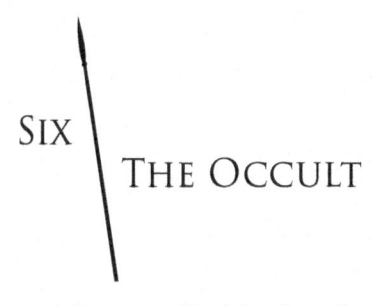

The word "occult" means "hidden" or "secret." Occult practices offer a path to knowledge and power through secret arts. While people often dabble with the occult, it is intended to be mastered by a specialist. These specialists are usually priests, magi, shamans, or witchdoctors, but anyone who learns the arts can gain access to the supernatural.

All occult systems follow a common model. That model can be understood as a pyramid. First, there are those inside the pyramid and those outside. Outsiders are considered "blind." Those who reach the top are considered "enlightened." One becomes an insider by going through a ritual. In most cases, this ritual involves some level of nakedness, a blindfold, a threat of death for revealing secrets, a confession of blindness, and a pledge of obedience to a master who will lead you to enlightenment by revealing secret knowledge that leads to secret power. Such stories have been told by many who have left organizations like Wicca, Freemasonry, and Satanic cults.

After initiation, occultists learn secrets of a craft that give them access to an increasing amount of knowledge and power. You can see the word *craft* in witchcraft. The degrees of Freemasonry provide one of the clearest examples of moving from initiation to mastery.

In a video called "I'll never go back," a former Amazonian shaman named Shoefoot tells his story of turning from the occult to Christ. While it is popular these days to romanticize tribal religion and shamanism, his story is revealing. He tells of his initiation and going deeper into the world of secret wisdom and power. At various stages he "invited spirits into his chest." These spirits gave him sight into the unseen realm and provided him with secret knowledge and secret power. After becoming a Christian, he told these spirits to leave and changed his name to Bautista ("Baptized One").[1] Stories from former occultists, Masons, Mormon leaders, Satanists, and witches all share the same similarities regarding initiation rituals and spiritual experiences.

The idea of a hidden path to power and secret knowledge has always appealed to those who crave power either because they are ambitious or because they feel powerless. It is very common to find young people interested in the occult who feel overlooked or beaten down by their peers. It gives them a sense of superiority over those who look down on them. Those in the occult often develop a prideful attitude that says, "If you only knew what I could do to you, you would treat me with more respect."

Occult knowledge

A common adage says that knowledge is power. How much would it be worth to know which decisions would lead to prosperity and which to disaster? How much would it be worth to learn the cure for a deadly illness? How much would you pay to learn the secrets that would give you an advantage in business, love, or war? In pagan societies priests and witchdoctors are often paid great sums of money to read the omens that reveal the secrets of the gods. This art is called divination. It is rooted in the idea that the gods (hence the word *divine* in divination) often reveal their secrets through omens which can be read if one has learned the sacred arts.

Ancient forms of divination included cutting open an animal and "reading" the positions of the organs. If all was

---

1 | "I'll never go back" can be found at https://vimeo.com/242249127

normal, it was taken as a good omen from the gods. If something was out of place or diseased, it boded evil. Modern forms of divination include Tarot cards, Ouija boards, tea leaves, and palm reading.

Common occult practices related to secret knowledge:

- Astrology/Horoscopes/Zodiac
- Séances
- Fortune Telling/Palm reading/Tarot cards
- Mind reading/Telepathy
- Reincarnation readings
- Channeling
- Spirit Guides
- Ouija Boards

Occult Power

The occult offers a variety of secret paths to power that have great appeal for those who want to feel like they are in control of their lives. Here is a list of common occult practices related to secret power.

- Spells and curses
- Sorcery
- Astral projection
- Levitation
- Automatic Writing

The paths to power can be divided into power symbols/objects, power words, and power rituals.

Power symbols/objects. Occult symbols generally have two or more meanings. They have a surface meaning that is meant to deceive or mislead the uninitiated, and they have a deeper, hidden meaning that is known to those with the secret knowledge. These symbols are often used to summon spirits. For example, an amulet is a power object that is often worn as a necklace. The amulet is normally covered with occult symbols or words that are intended to summon spirits of protection for the one who wears the amulet. This was a very common practice in the Roman Empire and continues to be practiced in the New Age movement today.

Another example of a power object is an idol or a sacred stone. In tribal cultures and ancient pagan civilizations, it was common for people to have a shrine in their home where they offered prayers to one or more deities. It was also common to place power objects in strategic places around the house or in the garden in order to summon protective spirits or spirits that granted fertility and blessing.

Power Words. Just as symbols and objects are used as channels for spiritual power, so words can be used this way. Spells, incantations, curses, and the like are used to summon spirits and invite them to unleash their powers. New Testament professor Clinton Arnold has done some excellent work explaining how the pagan ideas of the ancient world form the background for understanding Paul's teaching in the book of Ephesians.[2]

The first century converts to Christianity would have been steeped in overt paganism. Their lives would have been filled with power objects, power words, and power rituals. Their question was, "Now that we are Christians, how do we distance and protect ourselves from the spirits and where do we turn for blessing on our homes?" Ephesians answers this question. In Christ we have been given every spiritual

---

[2] See Clinton Arnold's commentaries on Ephesians and Colossians in the *Zondervan Illustrated Bible Backgrounds Commentary* vol. 5 (Grand Rapids: Zondervan, 2019) for more information on the occult worldview and activity of the Roman world.

blessing in the heavenly realms (1:3). Christians no longer need to go to this god for one blessing and another god for a different blessing. We no longer need to invoke certain power words or perform certain power rituals in order to find the protection and blessing we need. Jesus has been given a name above every name and a position far above all other principalities and powers.

Power Rituals. Witchcraft, sorcery, and pagan sacrifice all include rituals designed to summon spiritual power. The general idea is that the greater the sacrifice offered, the greater the power unleashed. This is why the priests and prophets of Baal and Asherah cut themselves with knives and made themselves bleed in their contest with Elijah on Mount Carmel (1 Kings 18:28). They believed the gods would take notice of the sacrifice and answer their prayers as a result. People who practice such rituals need to renounce their involvement with them and cancel the claims of the Enemy on their lives as a result of them. The prayers in "Step One" of Neil Anderson's *Steps to Freedom in Christ* provide a model to guide you through such a prayer.

I once interviewed a young man in India who had been a witchdoctor there. According to his testimony, his father was killed when an occultist put a curse on him. His mother's response was to pay his way to receive the training he needed to become an occultist and kill the man who had killed his father. As he deepened in his training, he performed increasingly dark sacrifices and spent a growing amount of time in trances, disconnected from this world and in the company of spirits from the unseen world. Finally, he asked one of the spirits what he had to do to kill his enemy. The spirit told him that an especially dark form of sacrifice was needed. He performed the ritual, and immediately the spirit left the circle for a few hours and returned. The next morning his enemy was found dead in his home. This was the turning point in the young man's story. His devotions to the dark arts had alienated him from all friendships. He was feared and avoided by all. Eventually, he turned to the Christians for help, and at first they did not want him. But a pastor took him in and led him to Christ. He went through deliverance of the spirits that laid claim to him; and when I met him, he was in seminary preparing to enter the ministry.

Syncretism and Christianity

One of the problems Christians face is the danger of syncretism. Syncretism is the unnatural blending of worldviews or cultural practices. In many communities in Europe where people were forced to adopt Christianity, the churches would be filled with Christian symbols inside the buildings but pagan symbols outside the buildings, because the people continued to believe that they needed their traditional protections from evil spirits. A pastor in Africa, who was running for the office of bishop in his denomination, went to the tribal witchdoctor to have a curse placed on his opponent in order to improve his chances of winning the election. This pastor could ace his theology tests, but when it came to questions of power, nothing had convinced him that the power of Christ could compete with the power of the tribal spirits.

Too much of what passes as Christian spirituality is actually dressed up paganism. You see this when people use their Bibles as power objects, believing they will be protected from evil spirits if they sleep with it or keep it in their pocket. Many Catholic items get used this way from rosaries to crucifixes to statues of the saints placed in the garden. These objects are treated the same way that a pagan would treat their power objects. You also see this in the prosperity gospel movement. Faith is often used like magic. If you want something, all you need to do is say the right words or provide the right offering, and God will give you what you want.

Syncretism with the occult can lead to counterfeit Christian experiences, which is why we need to learn how to test spirits. I have colleagues who have exposed and evicted demons related to the following:

- False tongues
- False visions
- False slaying in the spirit experiences
- False prophecies
- False healings

One missionary sent me an email about nine children who were all "slain in the Spirit" simultaneously at the altar of the church. All nine had the same vision which, on the surface, sounds like confirmation that this was a legit experience. In their visions they were taken to heaven and hell and given a tour. However, their visions taught a very clear theology of legalism. Christians who had danced or listened to Christian rock music were floating in lava. All sorts of other "sins" had consigned people to hell even though they had put their faith in Christ. In response to this email, I replied that I could not think of a better way of starting a cult than with a false vision like this. Many cults and splinter groups have formed around one person or a cluster of people whose words and visions are taken as authoritative.

I am not saying that all Charismatic gifts are counterfeit. On the contrary, if there was nothing authentic, there would be nothing to counterfeit. However, I have found that many Christians who operate in spiritual realities have not learned how to test for demonic counterfeits. This is where "if" prayers come in handy. As we noted earlier, an "if" prayer looks something like this:

"If this gift/experience I have had is from the Holy Spirit, I thank God for it and ask Him to help me use it for His glory. But if I have been deceived, and this is a demonic counterfeit, I renounce it in the name of Jesus and command every wicked spirit to leave now and take your works and effects with you."

The purpose of taking this dive into demons and the occult is not to increase fear or paranoia, but to give guidance on how to discern what is from the enemy and not from God. Every believer needs to know how to discern good from evil and authentic from counterfeit. Paul taught that signs and wonders validated the ministry of a true apostle (2 Corinthians 12:12) and the author of Hebrews wrote that the Gospel was confirmed by signs and wonders (2:4), but Paul also warned us that the devil can deceive us with "signs and wonders" (2 Thessalonians 2:9). Thus, there is a need for testing. Signs and wonders can support the truth, but they can also reinforce a lie.

Syncretism and Secularity

Not only can the occult be subtly entwined with Christian faith and practice, it is often blended with secularity. The New Age Movement is the most notable example of this. People often engage in occult practices but try to explain them scientifically. This is a big topic, but let me offer a couple of examples.

You may have heard people say that humans only use ten percent of our brain capacity with the implication that if we could "tap in" to the other 90% we could levitate objects (like Yoda or Luke Skywalker) and read people's minds. There is no science behind this. It is more like an urban legend. It is increasingly common among mental and physical health practitioners to employ occult practices without any awareness of the spiritual forces they are summoning. An increasing number of hospitals employ shamans and other occultists.

There are so many Eastern and tribal practices making their way into the scientific community that it can be confusing to know what is okay and what is not. This is where binding and testing can help. When I go to an appointment and the practitioners use techniques that are not based on established science but on the fact that they the work, I often bind demons silently and command that no demon will be allowed to take advantage of my ignorance. Afterward, I test and command that if anything attempted to transfer to me, it has to leave.

While in Europe a few years ago, I met with a lady who had gone through Reiki massage. I had not heard of it at the time, so we tested the spirits. She prayed, "If I opened a door to demons by participating in this, I renounce my sin in Jesus' name." I could see a clear distortion come over her face, and she reported hearing demonic thoughts in her head. She then commanded those spirits to leave and felt a new peace inside. Stories like this can be repeated among those who practice testing spirits.

RED – Renounce, End, Destroy

As we have seen, the CCC-C model is effective in removing permission and evicting wicked spirits. When it comes to dealing with occult-related sin, I recommend adding RED to this.

R – Renounce. Make a blanket renunciation of all occult involvement like this:

> "In the name of the Lord Jesus Christ, I renounce the devil and all of his works. I ask God to cancel all permission against me because of occult activity in which I have engaged knowingly or unknowingly."

Then begin to renounce specific ways in which you may have participated in the occult. You can use the lists in this chapter to get started or use Neil T. Anderson's *Steps to Freedom in Christ* step one: "Counterfeit vs. Real."

E – End memberships. If you have joined an occult group, if possible, end your membership. If you cannot do that safely, declare an end to your membership and ask God to enforce that declaration in heaven.

D – Destroy occult objects. In Acts 19 we read how the church in Ephesus destroyed thousands of dollars' worth of occult objects. It was common then, and it is still common in some circles, for people to trust in Christ for salvation but continue participating in the occult out of a perceived need for the safety and power it offers. This is not appropriate for Christians.

The rule of thumb I use on what needs to be destroyed is this: if the object was created or used for an occult purpose, destroy it. For example, idols, amulets, tarot cards, masonic paraphernalia, ritual items, or clothing. If the object is not normally associated with the occult but you suspect a curse has been placed on it, that curse can normally be revoked using the CCC-C process. The Holy Spirit may give you specific guidance regarding what needs to be destroyed and what can simply be cleansed.

Conclusion

A functional knowledge of spiritual warfare is one of the foundational pillars of a Christian worldview. It is as primary to our understanding of the Christian life as the sovereignty of God or our union with Christ. In fact, I would argue that these are the three core pillars on which all Christianity rests.

The first is our union with Christ, which deals with our death, resurrection, and ascension with Christ so that we now live our lives in Him and He in us. The second is the sovereignty of God, which teaches us that God is strong enough, wise enough, and good enough to use even the evil that exists and is done in this world to advance His eternal purposes for His people. Finally, there is spiritual warfare. This doctrine teaches us that when we were adopted spiritually into God's family, we became targets of God's archenemy. This enemy is actively working to make sure we do not live our lives on the foundation of the first two pillars.

This is where the Christian finds balance in the study of spiritual warfare. We need to know our enemy, understand his tactics, and be prepared to stand against him with the weapons of our warfare. But we do not live our lives focused on the enemy. We live our lives in union with Christ and by faith in the sovereignty of God. This is where our focus lies, and this is the path to a deeper walk with God. My prayer for you is that you will not be deceived by our adversary the devil, but will learn to enjoy the simplicity, freedom, and beauty of a deeper walk with Christ.

Discussion Questions

1. Summarize what you learned about the occult in this lesson.

2. What questions did this chapter raise for you? Where might you be able to start looking for some answers to those questions?

3. The occult can be obvious (witchcraft, etc.), but it can also be subtle. What are some obvious examples of occult activity that Christians should avoid? Name some subtle forms.

4. Where have you seen syncretism at work in our culture? What convinced you that a particular practice was syncretistic?

5. Now that you have completed the final chapter in this book, what have been the most helpful lessons you have gleaned through this study?

Personal Exercise

This is an exercise to gain freedom from past or present occult involvement.

Renounce

Review the following list of occult practices that seek power and knowledge from a spiritual source other than God. If you have participated in any of these activities or have objects related to them in your home, use the sample prayer to renounce your involvement.

Spells and curses

Sorcery

Astral projection

Levitation

Automatic writing

Astrology/Horoscopes/Zodiac

Séances

Fortune telling/Palm reading/Tarot cards

Mind reading/Telepathy

Reincarnation readings

Channeling

Spirit Guides

Ouija Boards

"In the name of the Lord Jesus Christ, I renounce the devil and all of his works. I ask God to cancel all permission against me because of occult activity in which I have engaged knowingly or unknowingly. I specifically renounce _____ *(list all areas in which you have engaged in the occult)* and command any demons who have had permission to a place in my life to leave now and go where the Lord Jesus Christ sends you."

End

Consider the list of possible occult organizations listed below and end your affiliation with the following prayer.

Wicca

Paganism

Covens

Cult groups

False religions

Freemasonry

Satanism

Other group that the Lord brings to mind: _____.

> "In the name of the true Lord Jesus Christ who came in the flesh, died, and rose again, I renounce my membership or participation in any group that practiced or taught occult secrets. I specifically choose to end my association with _____. I ask You, Father, to cancel any permission this has given to the enemy, and I command any wicked spirits that have been assigned to me to leave now and go where the Lord Jesus Christ sends you."

Destroy

If you still own objects used in occult practices, these should be destroyed—not taken to Goodwill or put in the trash. A hammer and a fire might be helpful. Ask a prayer partner to join you. Destroy the objects after praying prayers of renunciation. When you are finished, command any wicked spirits related to the objects to leave and go where the Lord Jesus sends them.

Commit

The following prayer from Mark Bubeck's workbook *Preparing for Battle* is a good way to wrap up your experience of ending occult involvement.

> Dear heavenly Father, I praise You that I am united with the Lord Jesus Christ in all of His life and work. By faith I desire to enter into the victory of the incarnation of my Lord today. I invite Him to live His victory in me. Thank You, Lord Jesus Christ, that You experienced all temptation that I experience and yet never sinned.
>
> I enter by faith into the mighty work of the crucifixion of my Lord. Thank You, dear Father, that through Jesus' blood there is moment-by-moment

cleansing from sin, permitting me to fellowship with You. Thank You that the work of the Cross brings Satan's work to nothing.

I enter by faith into the full power and authority of my Lord's resurrection. I desire to walk in the newness of life that is mine through my Lord's resurrection. Lead me into a deeper understanding of the power of the Resurrection. By faith I enter into my union with the Lord Jesus Christ in His ascension. I rejoice that my Lord displayed openly His victory over all powers as He ascended into glory through the very realm of the prince of the power of the air.

I enter into my victory aggressively and claim my place as more than a conqueror through Him who loves me. I offer up this prayer in the name of the Lord Jesus with thanksgiving. Amen.[3]

---

3 | Mark I. Bubeck, *Preparing for Battle: A Spiritual Warfare Workbook* (Chicago: Moody 1991) p. 235.

Appendices

APPENDIX 1

FREEDOM PRAYERS

Prayer for confessing and cancelling sin:

Lord Jesus Christ, I confess that I have been involved in _____. Please forgive me for this sin and misuse of my body and cancel any ground that the Enemy may claim because of this sin. I choose now to receive your forgiveness and in so doing to forgive myself, so that I will not remain in bondage to this sin any longer. Amen.

Prayer for evicting demons:

(Having removed all legal ground the Enemy may claim)

In the name of my Lord Jesus Christ and by the power of His blood, I bind together as one every demon assigned to me because of this sin, and command them all to leave. Lord Jesus, I ask you to send them where they will trouble me no more and to do whatever is necessary to enforce this eviction. Amen.

Prayer for binding the enemy during a renunciation:

In the name of my Lord Jesus Christ I bind any demon from in any way interfering with what Christ wants to do here today. I bind you to inactivity and to silence. You will not harm me or anyone in this room. You will not act out but will submit to whatever commands you are given as one who has been defeated by the blood of the Lord Jesus Christ.

Prayer for breaking soul ties:

In the name of my Lord Jesus Christ, I renounce any soul tie that has been formed between me and _____ through my _____. I cancel any demonic bond that keeps us connected and command those demons to leave now and go where the Lord Jesus sends you.

Prayer for choosing to forgive:

Lord Jesus Christ, I choose to forgive _____ for . . . *(list ways in which you have been hurt or wronged and the consequences it has created for you).*

Prayer for cancelling generational ground:

In the name of my Lord Jesus Christ, I cancel the legal ground surrendered by my ____ *(list specifics of what you know).* Here and now, I renounce any claim that any demons have on me, my children, or any other member of my family because of the sins of my ancestors. In the name of Jesus, I command every evil spirit assigned to me or my family as a result of these sins to leave now and go where the Lord Jesus sends you.

Prayer for cleansing a home:

In the name of my Lord Jesus Christ, I renounce any claim that any demons may have on this home *(or other property).* As one with authority over this home and as a child of the King, I renounce the sins that opened a door for any demonic presence in this place. Therefore, in the name of Jesus, I command every demon to leave this place now and go where my Lord Jesus Christ sends you. And now, I invite the Holy Spirit to sweep this place clean and fill it with His presence. I ask that the blessing and peace of God will rest on this place so that it may be a haven of rest, a home blessed by God.

In Jesus' name, Amen.

Appendix 2

Theological Note: The Role of Experience

In the practice of spiritual warfare ministry a lot is learned and tested by experience. This does not mean that our theology is built on experience. Our theology is built on Scripture. However, at some level all theology is informed by experience. No human can truthfully claim to be entirely free of the effects of their experience. In fact, the functional worldview that comprises our true, heart-level beliefs about life is largely formed before we are old enough to know what a worldview is.

Not long ago I read that the average child has a fully functioning worldview developed by the age of five. Our worldview is shaped far more by the relational and cultural patterns of our experience than it is by reason, logic, and words. Our worldview helps us interpret our experiences and creates our innate sense of "the way things really are" and "the way things really work."

Our worldview with its presuppositions and assumptions about life forms a filter through which we read the Bible and interpret experience. Most pastors and theologians who have been raised and trained in Western cultures don't realize how thoroughly the scientific worldview has impacted them. Their worldview lenses often keep them from recognizing the spiritual warfare around them for what it is, because it gets explained as something else.

In the first century there was one group who had their theological system established, and no experience was allowed to challenge it. They were the Pharisees. There was no room in their theological framework for their experience of

Jesus and the kinds of things He was doing. However, their experience of Jesus was meant to challenge their theology and drive them back to the Scriptures to re-examine their old model and develop a new model.

At the Jerusalem Council (Acts 15), Peter appealed to his experience with Cornelius as confirmation of his interpretation of Scripture which said that the church needed to include Gentiles. Several times in Acts, Paul appealed to his experience on the Damascus Road to validate his ministry. In his letter to the Galatians he appealed to his own experience of divine revelation as the foundation of his authority. He also appealed to the church's experience of receiving the Holy Spirit in response to faith rather than works as confirmation of his message of justification by grace alone.

When it comes to the question of whether or not a Christian can have a demon, there is no Scripture that says it cannot happen, and there are biblical models that describe how it can occur (such as the temple model described in Ezekiel and Nehemiah). The New Testament authors describe the possibility of Christians giving "ground" to the devil (Ephesians 4:27), of needing to take thoughts captive and tear down strongholds (2 Corinthians 10:5), and of falling into the "snare of the devil" (2 Timothy 2:26). We are warned to "be alert,"[1] "stand firm,"[2] resist,"[3] "watch and pray,"[4] and to "put on the whole armor of God."[5] Such Scriptures suggest that Christians are in a very real war with an enemy that wants to destroy them. We are warned to be on guard and to be prepared for conflict with the devil. We

---

[1] | 1 Peter 5:8

[2] | Ephesians 6:14

[3] | James 4:7; 1 Peter 5:9

[4] | Matthew 26:41

[5] | Ephesians 6:11, 13

are warned that it is possible to give him ground and fall into his snares. We are told to resist him.

The idea that Christians have immunity from demonic oppression is never taught in Scripture. Rather, we are taught the basis of our victory over the devil and encouraged to use the weapons of our warfare to fight against him. With this scriptural background, we have a foundation for dealing with those situations in which Christians have indeed found themselves losing their battle with the enemy. Add to this the experiences of a growing number of evangelicals who have found freedom from spiritual bondage through the application of spiritual warfare principles such as those taught in this book, and the evidence becomes overwhelming.

Most people who reject the idea that Christians can be demonized have either had negative experiences with people misapplying warfare principles or they have had no experience at all. Unfortunately, I know of many cases of people who have given spiritual warfare ministry a bad name by the silly and sometimes damaging things they have done while attempting to do "deliverance." Too often, these people do not have a biblically-balanced approach to warfare and they do not learn how to test the spirits. Therefore, they get caught up in all sorts of practices that are themselves occult in nature or simply foolish.

On the other hand, I know of many pastors who began their ministries by denying that Christians could be demonized and arguing strenuously against people like Mark Bubeck, Fred Dickason, Tim Warner, and Neil Anderson. Yet many of these same pastors now embrace the teachings of such Bible teachers, because they have had firsthand experiences of seeing family members and close personal friends set free. It is easier to reject this teaching when you are not faced with a demonized colleague or family member who desperately needs your help.

One of the reasons that some people have so few experiences with demonic encounters is that they lack the worldview lenses to recognize what they are seeing. Their approach to the Bible and to Christianity is more Western than they realize. They have been trained to see natural explanations first, and to consider supernatural explanations only as a last resort.

It would seem reasonable to say that the best theological system is the one that is rooted in Scripture and confirmed by experience. This is what we have tried to do at Deeper Walk. Our study and our experience have led us to the conclusion that Christians can be demonized and may need to go through "deliverance" from these demons. There have been many who have opposed this teaching, but after thousands of cases of Christians experiencing deliverance from the demonic and a solid biblical explanation for what is happening, perhaps it is time to turn the page on this debate and get focused on equipping ministry leaders to help people in a biblically-balanced way.

Throughout history medical breakthroughs capable of helping millions often met with resistance from the establishment. Louis Pasteur's theory of bacteria and germ-based disease was widely condemned as "junk science" by his peers.[6] He was condemned as a fraud and a menace to "true" science. But within a generation his new, "heretical" ideas had become standard practice. It is time for seminaries and Bible colleges around the country to realize what a wonderful resource this type of ministry has to offer and get on the leading edge of preparing its pastors and leaders to engage in spiritual warfare ministry with solid, biblically-anchored training that will enable them to approach this area of ministry with competence and understanding.

---

6 | Agnes Ullmann, "Louis Pasteur: French Chemist and Microbiologist: at Brittanica.com. https://www.britannica.com/biography/Louis-Pasteur/Research-career

Most Evangelicals avoid the subject of spiritual warfare or at least minimize the role of demons as a functional part of life. But why? Why is this topic so neglected? Here are five common reasons people often avoid the subject of spiritual warfare.

1. **Fear** – Some people are afraid that if they study spiritual warfare, creepy things will start happening to them. I actually had a theology professor tell us not to study spiritual warfare because weird things always happened around his house when he began preparing to teach on demonology. However, I tend to think that is a reason to learn about spiritual warfare, not avoid it.

2. **Anecdotes** – Many people have heard stories of Christians who have gone off the deep end in their fascination with spiritual warfare. I admit, you don't have to look far to find examples of this. Of course, this is the same argument used by many people who won't consider the claims of Christ. The Christians they know aren't much of a testimony for the message they embrace. This doesn't mean it is wise to ignore Christianity, nor is it a valid reason to ignore spiritual warfare.

3. **Controversy** – I had an executive pastor tell me that he would welcome my Bible survey and discipleship training at his church but that he would not allow me to do a seminar on spiritual warfare. He was quite open about his reason. It was not that he disagreed with what I would teach, but that the subject was considered controversial and he didn't want to ruffle any feathers.

4. **Theology** – There are respected Bible scholars who teach that Christians can't have demons. They see the presence of the Holy Spirit within as a sort of

vaccination or forcefield against demonic activity. Their theological systems lead them to oppose those who write books like this that offer specific guidance for Christians who have an internal battle with demons.

5. **Secularity** - Western Christians tend to live with a worldview that makes demons and demonic activity seem remote and unlikely to affect them. They often assume that if they don't go poking around in the snake's pit, the snakes won't bother them. As a leading Christian psychologist wrote,

> I have had hundreds of patients who came to see me because they thought they were demon possessed.... I discovered that all of the 'demons' I was seeing were allergic to Thorazine and that, in nearly every case, a week or two on Thorazine made the 'demons' go away."[7]

The Thorazine may have helped the symptoms, but in cases of genuine demonization, it is not a lasting solution. I can guarantee you that this psychologist had clients with very real demons. I know of people who helped some of his former clients find freedom from these wicked spirits. The problem was that his secularized thinking kept him from accurately diagnosing what he was experiencing. Lack of training in this area, also kept him from knowing what to do about it.

I would argue that most of the reasons people avoid the topic of spiritual warfare can be turned around to make a strong case for why we need good, balanced, practical teaching on how to deal with demons.

---

7 | Korem and Meier, *The Fakers* (Baker, 1980) p. 162

- **Fear.** Are Christians afraid of spiritual warfare? Could some of that fear be due to ignorance? Since we are taught to wear armor, stand, resist, and fight the good fight, does it not make more sense to get trained in battle?
- **Anecdotes.** Everything can get out of balance. The Bible mishandled can be used in abusive ways. Pastoral care done without understanding can do damage. Warfare principles can be misapplied, and problems can be blamed on demons when that is not the issue. But when you have a warfare problem, only a warfare solution will work.
- **Controversy.** There is no Christianity without controversy. Jesus was a very controversial figure. It took real courage to oppose the synagogue leaders who called Him a heretic. There was significant pressure within the religious community to avoid Jesus. We always have to determine whether or not the good outweighs the bad when it comes to dealing with controversy.
- **Theology.** Theology lives at the intersection of Scripture and experience. Sometimes experiences challenge our theology and cause us to take a second look at our interpretations. Jesus was rejected by the Pharisees because they would not allow the experience of His signs and wonders to challenge their theology. While experience should never contradict Scripture, it often needs to challenge our interpretations.
- **Secularity.** In *The Solution of Choice,* Jim Wilder and I detail the impact secularity has had on the church and how it has affected the solutions we offer to people in need. While biblical teachers are not secular and would oppose it as a worldview, many have been more influenced by it than they realize when it comes to interpreting and applying the text.

Christians often get bad advice from Bible teachers, and this leaves them helpless at a time when Satan's assault on the church is reaching epic proportions. My father, Timothy Warner, put it this way:

> Our first priority is to know God, but if we are really at war with a clever, experienced enemy, we need to know as much as we can about him. . . . Not to know how your enemy thinks and how he acts is to give your enemy a strategic advantage over you.[1]

---

[1] Timothy M. Warner, *Spiritual Warfare* (Crossway, 1991) p. 27.

APPENDIX 3

MARK BUBECK'S ROUND-UP PRAYER

I worship and honor my heavenly Father, the Lord Jesus Christ and the Holy Spirit; the true and living God Who promised, "I will never leave you or forsake you." I welcome and honor the unseen presence of my Lord Jesus Christ who promised always to be with us when we meet in His name. I honor and thank You, Lord Jesus Christ, for Your invisible presence in this very place with us. I ask You to be in charge and to affect only Your will and plan in our lives. I yield fully to Your will in the eviction of any and all wicked spirit control from my life. I desire the Holy Spirit to do the sanctifying work within my whole person and being that He is there to do.

I ask You, Lord Jesus Christ, to assign Your holy angels to protect us from any strategies of darkness designed to oppose this prayer for freedom. Keep Satan and all his opposing hosts of evil away from us. I also ask You to ensure that wicked spirits evicted from my presence will depart quickly and directly to the place where You consign them to go.

In the Name of my Lord Jesus Christ and by the power of His blood, I affirm my authority over all wicked spirits assigned to control me and hinder my life and witness for Christ. I now command all lingering wicked spirits assigned to harass, rule and control me to cease their work and be bound in the presence of the Lord Jesus Christ. I bind in all back-up systems and replacer wicked spirits assigned to rebuild evicted strongholds. They may not do that! I command all those spirits assigned against me to be and remain whole spirits. I forbid any dividing, restructuring or multiplying of wicked spirit activity against me.

There is to be one-way traffic of evil spirit activity out of my life and to the place the Lord Jesus Christ consigns them. I pull in from other family members all those wicked spirits working under the chain of authority established by the powers of darkness assigned to rule over me. I command them all to be bound together here in the presence of my Lord Jesus Christ in that spiritual realm where He dwells with me and they know His presence. I bind all of your wicked ears open and it is my will that you must hear and obey Him who is your Creator and Conqueror.

I declare the Lord Jesus Christ to be my Redeemer and Lord. I affirm that God has seated me with Christ Jesus in the heavenly realms far above all principalities and supernatural powers of darkness and evil. Lord Jesus Christ, I ask You to tell all of these powers of darkness assigned to afflict and rule over me where they must go. I want them out of my life and confined where they can never trouble me again.

I yield fully to Your sovereign plan for my life and all of the purposes You have in this battle I have been facing. I ask You, Lord Jesus Christ, to tell them clearly where they must go.

(A brief pause is in order to honor the Lord Jesus Christ's work of addressing His authority and victory against those powers of darkness bound in accountability before Him.)

I now ask the Holy Spirit dwelling within my person to affect the will of the Lord Jesus Christ concerning these afflicting powers of darkness. Just as You forced them out of people's lives in response to Jesus' commands when He walked on this earth, I ask You to accomplish that for me now. I ask You, Spirit of the living God, to evict from my conscious, sub-conscious and unconscious mind all control of any wicked powers. Break all of their power and control over my thought processes. They must go where the Lord Jesus Christ sends them. Sweep them away and make my mind clear of any wicked spirit control.

I now ask that the Holy Spirit would renew and sanctify my mind. Cleanse and take full control of my conscious, unconscious and sub-conscious mind, precious Holy Spirit. Set it totally apart for the Glory of God and the service of my Lord Jesus Christ. I deliberately yield my mind to the Lordship of Christ, the truth of God's Word and the will of my heavenly Father.

I now ask that the Holy Spirit would look all through my emotions on the conscious, sub-conscious and unconscious level. Evict any controlling Powers of darkness and may the holy angels escort them to the place where the Lord Jesus Christ is commanding them to go. Clean them out and totally away from my person.

I ask that the gracious Holy Spirit would take control of my emotions on every level of the function of my feelings. Sanctify my emotions. Fill my emotions with the Spirit's fruit, love, joy, peace, patience, gentleness, meekness, faithfulness and self-control. I welcome the Holy Spirit's internal control of my feelings. I look to the Spirit of God to sanctify and renew my emotions. I reach out to experience the Lord's plan for my emotional freedom and spiritual well-being.

I now ask that the Holy Spirit would look all through my conscious, unconscious and sub-conscious will for any control of wicked powers. Evict them now to where the Lord Jesus Christ is commanding them to go. Sweep my will totally clean from evil control and manipulation. May the Holy Spirit of the true and living God renew and sanctify my will fully for the glory of God. Will within me to do the will of God. May the Lordship of Jesus Christ be obediently lived out in my life by the Holy Spirit's full control of my will.

I offer my body in all of its parts and functions as an expression of my spiritual worship to You. I ask that You would have the Holy Spirit to look through my body for any controlling activity of wicked spirits and all through my brain for any fallen spirit's affliction or control. Evict them totally away from this physical control center for the function of my mind and body. I offer my brain and its capacities for the quickening, renewing control of the Holy Spirit. Sanctify and refresh my brain so that it functions in spiritual harmony with Your control of my whole person. Look all through the senses of my body and sever any wicked spirit control of my eyes, ears, smell, touch or taste. Look all through the organs of my body for any defiling work of the kingdom of darkness. Sanctify my body organs and their function by the quickening work of the Holy Spirit. I ask You to look all through the sexual organs and function of my body for any evil spirit activity. Set apart my sexuality for Your glory and for Your Holy plan of moral purity and sexual intimacy only in the bonds of marriage. I ask that the Holy Spirit would search out all my bones, blood circulation, nerve circuitry, muscles, tissues, glands, hair, skin, and every cell for any wicked spirit activity against my physical body. Evict any afflicting, evil powers totally away from my body. Sanctify my body in all of its parts and wholeness. I want my body to be a "holy body" not only in its standing in Your redemptive plan, but also in its function as a part of my spiritual worship to You. I offer my body as a living sacrifice to be used only for all that is acceptable in Your sight.

I now yield up my whole person again to You, the true and living God, and to Your full control and to the control of Your Son and Holy Spirit. I thank You for the freedom that You have affected within me during this time of prayer. I now look to the love of my heavenly Father, the lordship of Jesus Christ, and by the intercessions of the Holy Spirit to enable me to daily walk in the spiritual freedom promised me in God's holy Word. I reject, resist and refuse anything less. In the name and worthiness of my Lord Jesus Christ and by the intercessions of the Holy Spirit, I place these petitions before You, my Father in Heaven. ...AMEN

About the Author

Dr. Marcus Warner is the president of Deeper Walk International. A graduate of Trinity Evangelical Divinity School (M.Div., Th. M., D. Min.), Dr. Warner taught Old Testament and Theology at Bethel University in Mishawaka, Indiana and later served for seven years as the senior pastor of an evangelical church in Carmel, Indiana. He has over thirty years of experience in spiritual warfare ministry.

About Deeper Walk International

Deeper Walk International (formerly ICBC) has been providing biblically-balanced training in spiritual warfare ministry for over thirty years. The organization was founded by **Dr. Mark Bubeck**, author of the books *The Adversary* and *Overcoming the Adversary* (re-released as *Spiritual Warfare Prayer*) by Moody Publishers. ICBC quickly hired **Dr. Jim Logan**, author of *Reclaiming Surrendered Ground*, to be its first biblical counselor and **Dr. Dan Rumberger** to be its resident psychologist.

As time passed, new counseling centers were started, and new alliances were formed. **Dr. Timothy Warner** (my father), became the director of the Institute for Biblical Counseling. Dr. Warner co-authored *The Essential Guide to Spiritual Warfare* with Neil T. Anderson[1] and served as the director of the professional doctoral programs at Trinity Evangelical Divinity School during the 1980s.

---
1 | Neil T. Anderson and Timothy M. Warner, *The Essential Guide to Spiritual Warfare* (Grand Rapids: Baker, 2018) was originally released as *The Beginner's Guide to Spiritual Warfare.*

Today Deeper Walk provides training and resources related to heart-focused discipleship.

Other books by Dr. Marcus Warner include

- *Building Bounce* with Stefanie Hinman
- *The 4 Habits of Joy-Filled Marriages* with Chris Coursey
- *The Solution of Choice* with Jim Wilder
- *Slaying the Monster*
- *Rare Leadership* with Jim Wilder
- *Understanding the Wounded Heart*
- *The Spirit-Filled Home*
- *A Deeper Walk Guide to Advent*
- *How to Grow Joy*
- *REAL Prayer*
- *A D.I.D. Primer*
- *3-2-1 Bible Study Method*
- *Toward a Deeper Walk*
- *The Deeper Walk Guide to the Bible*

This book is intended to serve as a summary of the core elements of the biblically-sound approach to spiritual warfare that has characterized this ministry.

Go Deeper

Recommended Reading

The Essential Guide to Spiritual Warfare
Timothy Warner & Neil T. Anderson

The Adversary
Mark I. Bubeck

Warfare Praying
Mark I. Bubeck

Spiritual Warfare Prayers
Mark I. Bubeck

Spiritual Warfare
Karl Payne

Victory in Spiritual Warfare
Tony Evans

The Invisible War
Chip Ingram

The Bondage Breaker
Neil T. Anderson

The Steps to Freedom in Christ
Neil T. Anderson

Waking the Dead
John Eldredge

The Unseen Realm
Michael S. Heiser

Angels Elect and Evil
C. Fred Dickason

APPRECIATIONS

This book began as a summary of what I had learned from some significant mentors related to spiritual warfare ministry. It is only appropriate that I pause to acknowledge the fact that without them I would not have started this journey or written this book.

First and foremost are my dad and mom—Timothy and Eleanor Warner—who modeled well the idea that you could be a normal person and live a normal life and still engage in spiritual warfare ministry. Your world didn't have to become all about spiritual warfare in order to incorporate it into your life. I also learned from them by sitting in on many sessions and watching the maturity with which they interacted with people in need.

Along the way, I had the honor of reading books and then meeting people who became friends. Mark Bubeck (*The Adversary* and *Warfare Praying*), Fred Dickason (*Angels: Elect and Evil*), and Karl Payne (*Spiritual Warfare: Christians, Demonization, and Deliverance*) have all influenced my life in positive ways and provided a biblically-balanced foundation for this work.

A special thank you is also in order for my daughter, Stephanie, who persistently but gently urged me to complete the rewrite of this book and served as its editor. I think she worked harder on this than I did. She makes her dad very proud.

understanding the wounded heart
second edition

MARCUS WARNER

the world wounds us

the devil lies to us

we vow never to let it happen again

we spend our lives picking the fruit of our wounds

It doesn't have to stay this way.

This and other resources can be found at
www.DeeperWalkInternational.org

Deeper Walk
INTERNATIONAL

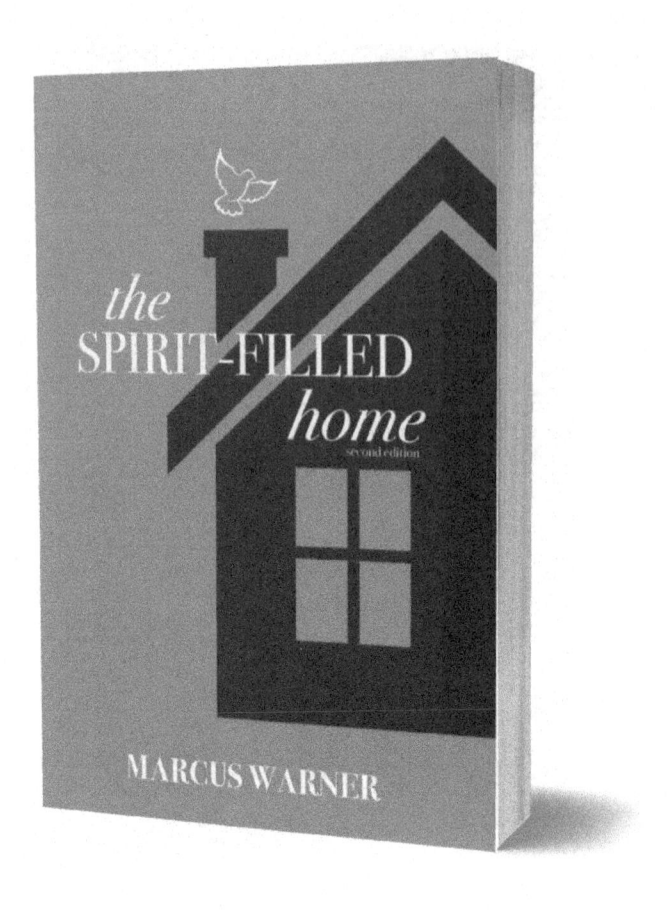

Flesh-filled homes breed conflict and pain.

Spirit-filled homes grow the maturity to handle hard things in loving ways.

This and other resources can be found at
www.DeeperWalkInternational.org

Deeper Walk
INTERNATIONAL

BUILDING BOUNCE
how to grow emotional resilience

MARCUS WARNER | STEFANIE HINMAN

Life is hard.

We all get overwhelmed at times.

But some people seem to bounce back from their upset emotions faster than most.

Are they just born happy?

Or is there **a secret to building emotional resilience that anyone can learn?**

This and other resources can be found at
www.DeeperWalkInternational.org

Deeper Walk
INTERNATIONAL